SIE

CW00815957

A BODY UN

WRITTEN BY DAVID LEWIS & PETER HUGHMAN
AND EDITED BY STEVE WRAITH

Mojo Risin'
Publishing Ltd

Published in 2020 by Mojo Risin' Publishing Ltd
www.mojorisinpublishing.com

British Library Cataloguing in Publication Data:
A catalogue record for this book is available from
the British Library

ISBN-13:
978-1-9163867-2-3

Cover design
David Stanyer

Layout
Neil Jackson, Media Arts
www.media-arts.co.uk

Printed & bound by PrintGuy
Proudly published Up North

Acknowledgements

We gratefully acknowledge the extensive help given, and original research conducted by author and film maker Neil Jackson, director of Footsteps in the Snow, a landmark documentary on the case.

We also thank the following: Steven Matthews, LLB, LLM,MA Dip AML, MICA, Michael Luvaglio, Dennis Stafford, Bertrand Russell; Christopher Farley; Graham Andrews; Joe Stafford; Francis and Maude Luvaglio; L. J. Pearce, Managing Director of Churchills (Gunmakers) Ltd; Professor Francis Camps; The Northern Forensic Science Laboratory; George Bowman (Jaguar Cars); The Governors' and staff of Wakefield and Parkhurst Prisons; James Golden; Thomas Leak; Thomas Oxley; Mauro Ferri; Alan Wood; James Bradbury; Thomas Purvis; Alexander Howie; Stanley Simpson; Selena Jones; Pat Burgess; Lilian Bunker; Gladys Hill; Pat Morgan, Robert Anderson; Dorothy Brady; Thomas Feather; Nora Burnip and Matthew Dean.

Photos: Neil Jackson - Media-Arts, Durham Police Authority, Cowan and Wilson (Sunderland), David Lewis-Hodgson Archive (www.thewayitwas.uk); Michael Luvaglio family album. Graphics: Goran Tovic.

Introduction
The Death of a Fruit Machine Man

'Murder most foul as of the best it is, but this most foul, strange and unnatural.'
William Shakespeare, Hamlet, Act 1 Scene 5

Early one bleak January morning, in 1967, a miner returning home from the night shift, came across a snow-covered Mark X Jaguar abandoned in the small Durham village of South Hetton. Its front had collision damage, the rear off-side window was shattered, and the body of a murdered man lay on the back seat. The victim was Angus Stuart Sibbet. A collector of money from One-Armed Bandits, had been shot three times at close range.

That afternoon, detectives drove to a small re-spraying firm in Sunderland and took possession of a red E-Type sports car. That night they arrested Dennis Stafford and Michael Luvaglio who both worked, like Sibbet himself, for Durham based Social Club Services. This successful and extremely wealthy gambling and entertainments empire was run by Vince Landa, Michael's older brother.

Michael, a close and long-time friend of the dead man, took care of the finances, Dennis booked acts for clubs and Angus collected money from the hundreds of Fruit Machines installed by the company in working men's clubs throughout the North East.

The two men had no motive for killing their friend and little opportunity for doing so. There were no forensic links between them, the dead man and the crime scene. The medical evidence regarding time of death was dubious and the murder weapon was never found.

The only connection between the three men was the Mark X, driven by Angus Sibbet, and the E-Type driven by Dennis Stafford had apparently been involved in a collision on the night of the murder. It was the mute testimony of these two vehicles alone that sent Michael Luvaglio and Dennis Stafford to jail for life.

According to the prosecution, damage to the front of the saloon and rear of the sports car, had been caused when they collided immediately prior to Sibbet's shooting. Their case, a complicated one it is fair to say, was based on a carefully selected items from a mass of evidence. Anything that might cast doubt on the prosecution case was either disregarded or suppressed. For example, the man who actually discovered the body was initially not going to be called as a witness because his testimony tended to discredit medical opinion about time of death.

As a detective story, the murder of Angus Sibbet makes compelling reading. A bitterly cold, moonless, winter's night. The snow-covered streets of a down-at-heel mining village. A luxury saloon with a dead man's bullet ridden corpse slumped on the bloodstained leather of the back seat. Footsteps in the snow leading away from the murder scene. A baffling crime with many witnesses providing deeply contradictory and conflicting testimony.

Introduction
How We Became Involved

In October 1969, an elderly couple knocked on the door of No. 10 Downing Street and handed in a petition. It asked the then Prime Minister, Harold Wilson, to set up an inquiry into the case. Delivered by Stafford's parents, it was another round in the fight by the two men, and their families, to secure a retrial or at least some official re-examination of the case. A report of their Downing Street visit found its way into an editorial conference at the Fleet Street news agency where I was working as an investigative journalist. My editor asked me to look into the story with a view to the possibility of an article on the case.

After interviewing Joe Stafford and reading the trial documents, I became disturbed by the inconsistencies, improbabilities and impossibilities of the prosecutions' case. I passed the papers to my friend, Peter Hughman, a rising young criminal lawyer, for his opinion. He too became as interested in and perturbed by the trial as I had been. We decided that the complexities and social importance of the subject demanded book-length treatment rather than the brief space and short life afforded by a magazine article.

In January 1970, by coincidence on the anniversary of the crime, we drove up to Newcastle-upon-Tyne to conduct interviews with witnesses. These included the many miners who had walked past the Mark X at different times in the night, those first on the murder scene, local residents and the few police officers prepared to talk to us, even off the record. We also had lengthy discussions with Graham Andrews, Dennis Stafford's solicitor.

The only people we did not immediately speak to were Dennis Stafford and Michael Luvaglio. This was deliberate policy on our part, as we decided from the start not to have any personal contact with them until after the book was written.

We wanted an entirely objective appraisal of the evidence. For the same reason we note here, and not elsewhere in the book, that in the course of our inquiries we met many people who had known both Dennis Stafford and Michael Luvaglio for months, in some cases years. Whilst of no evidential value, we were inevitably impressed by the fact that, without exception, they believed the men to be innocent.

When we finally visited them in prison, Michael at Wakefield and Dennis in Parkhurst on the Isle of Wight, the two men's markedly different personalities were immediately apparent.

Michael, who had never previously been in trouble with the law, was pale and thin, broken by his years behind bars. Dennis, for whom going to prison was almost an occupational hazard, was very much in command of his surroundings.

In the very snug and comfortable prison officer's lounge, where we conducted the interview rather than in the drab and formal visitors' room, a

Introduction

friendly warden officer brought us tea, in china crockery, plus a plate full of iced fancy cakes. After we'd been chatting for a while, an animated and completely relaxed Stafford asked if we'd like a some more tea. When he said we would, he snapped a finger at the nearest officer and said, in a voice which was more an instruction than a request.

'Drop more boiling water in the pot, Jimmy'. Here was a man who felt entirely in control of events. A little later Ronnie Kray came up to offer us further cake.

I had just recovered from mumps which, as an adult, can cause all sorts of disagreeable and painful side effects. I mention this to Ronnie who grinned as he told me. 'I knew a man who died of mumps.'

Hesitant to contradict one of Britain's most notorious gangsters, I politely mentioned that I didn't think you could die of mumps.

'You can if you give it to me,' said Ronnie without a trace of a smile on his face.

Peter agreed to represent Dennis Stafford at the Appeal and commissioned a private detective and a Chartered Surveyor to investigate police claims. Reports of their findings are included in this book.

In 1971, Penguin published Most Unnatural, our first book on the trial. The campaign it launched, supported by such influential figures as Lord Longford and Bertrand Russell, proved successful. Reginald Maudling, the Conservative Home Secretary, referred the convictions back to the Court of Appeal. Sadly, despite a mass of fresh evidence being produced by defence lawyers, Lord Chief Justice Widgery dismissed the appeal. Subsequent appeals and investigations proved equally unsuccessful in overturning the verdict. The two men remained behind bars for twelve years. More than 50 years later, they continue to protest their innocence.

In 1971, we encountered a number of legal obstacles prior to publication. Much of what we knew, and wanted to say, was considered too risky to publish. Those we suspected of involvement in the killing were still alive and the British legal system, with its punitive libel laws, made the threat too great.

Half a century later all that has changed. Most of those involved are now dead and a great deal of new evidence, and several previously suppressed documents, has been uncovered. Now for the first time we are able to tell the full story of two young London brothers who became vastly wealthy in 'sixties Newcastle. Within a few years of fleeing London and threats from the Krays, they created a gambling and nightclub empire valued at £35 million in today's money. An empire which came crashing to earth, in a matter of weeks, after one founding brother had been sentenced to life imprisonment and the other had fled abroad to escape arrest.

Our story is set in a city rife with corruption and the vicious gang warfare which erupted following the passing of the 1960 Betting and Gaming Act. We describe the part played, in the Newcastle's club scene, by such major villains as the Krays and Arthur Thompson, Glasgow's 'Godfather' of crime.

Introduction
Solve the Murder and Win £50,000

For more than half a century this murder has baffled some of the world's sharpest and most experienced legal minds.
Can you solve it and name the guilty man?

This book provides all the written and spoken evidence, police photographs, forensic and medical reports presented at the trial, our especially commissioned and never before published reports plus new facts unearthed by our own investigations.

We have suggested a possible solution based on years of research and detailed interviews with most of those involved. But we could be wrong! Which is why we are challenging you, our readers, to evaluate the evidence we provide, decide what can be relied upon and what needs to be discarded in order to work out how exactly the killing took place. As you will discover, not everything stated by witnesses, presented by experts or reported by the detectives can be correct.

If you can identify the killer and explain how the murder took place, then you could win the £50,000 reward currently being offered by Michael Luvaglio for information that leads directly to his conviction being overturned at a new appeal. For full details go to www.villain-or-victim.com.

Chapter One: A Body Under The Bridge

'Murder? No, I never thought it were murder - never in the world. Things like that don't happen in South Hetton.' Tom Leak

Early on the morning of 5 January 1967, Durham miner Tom Leak opened the rear door of a Mark X Jaguar and came face to face with a murder victim. The dead man was Angus Stuart Sibbet, a fruit machine collector. He had been shot three times at close range and dumped on the back seat of his brand-new car.

Sibbet's bloodied head rested against the rear offside door. Fragments of glass, from the shattered rear window, were scattered over his muddied clothes. Snow covered the car and flakes, blown in through the broken window by a stiff north-easterly wind, glistened in the yellow-orange glare of a nearby sodium streetlamp.

It had started snowing shortly after midnight and, by five o'clock that grim winter's day, heavy flurries driven before a bitterly cold north-easterly wind, had filled the narrow streets and back yards of the little Durham mining village of South Hetton. It had piled in sooty drifts against the close-boarded fences, collected on the roofs of grey stone houses and slate roofed colliery buildings.

Although surrounded by flat, thorn-hedged, fields and farms, the village located eighteen miles south-east of Newcastle-upon-Tyne, did not look rural. Where other country villages might boast an elegant church spire and quiet country lanes, sixties South Hetton was dominated by the mine's metal lift gantry, a steel mineral railway bridge and busy A 182 main road.

Because the 120-year-old colliery's 1,500 employees worked three shifts, the village never slept. Night and day, scores of miners filled the pavements coming on or going off shift. For over a century, the high-quality coal these miners dug from deep underground was the only reason why outsiders would have ever been aware of the little village's existence.

On that freezing cold January morning this would change for ever.

Tom Leak Finds a Body
At the age of eighteen, rather than follow his father and grandfather into the pit, Tom Leak joined up and served with the regular army for ten years. On returning to South Hetton he found work at the colliery. As a shot-firer his job involved using high explosives to bring down the hundreds of tons of coal for his fellow miners loaded onto conveyor belts. It was highly skilled and responsible work. A mistake on his part meant putting dozens of lives at risk.

A few days before we met him, Tom had been crawling through filthy, ice-cold, water with only a bobbing helmet lamp to light his way along a two-foot-high tunnel to inspect a roof fall. Despite the danger and discomfort, his training and well-disciplined nerves had enabled him to observe accurately and make a detailed and reliable report on the damage. It is important to keep in mind the sort of man Tom Leak is when considering what he observed that

7

morning, his friends were nowhere to be seen. Assuming, mistakenly, they had gone ahead he set off at a brisk pace to catch up.

A narrow track led from the colliery to the A182 which, as it passes through this part of South Hetton, is known as Front Street. To get to his house nearby Tom had to walk under what was known locally as Pesspool Bridge. Built 120 years earlier but modernised and widened in the early sixties, the steel-girdered bridge carried trains transporting the thousands of tons of coal the colliery produced daily.

When he neared the bridge, Tom saw a new Mark X saloon parked about fourteen inches from the kerb. Sodium streetlamps illuminated the dark green vehicle whose bonnet, rear window, and part of the roof covered with a thick layer of snow. At first, he believed the car had been left without lights. Later he noticed they were switched on but only the side lights were still glowing dimly. His first thought was that the car had been abandoned after running out of petrol.

Other miners, who passed the vehicle earlier that night, offered a cruder explanation. They had joked it must belong to the wealthy client of a prostitute who lived a few doors away. Tom read the registration number, MUP 11D and attempted to peer through the rear window, but the snow covering was too thick. Cupping his hands, he squinted into the near-side passenger window. Although the streetlight barely penetrated the saloon's interior, he was able to make out a man stretched across the back seat. He seemed to be asleep or ill. It never crossed Tom's mind he was dead.

The rear, near-side, door was jammed partly open by a piece of cloth. Ex-soldier Tom described it to us as 'left at half-cock.' Pulling the door open he saw the man was lying across the back seat, with his feet facing towards Tom. His clothes, dark suit, white shirt and shortie overcoat, were rumpled and, like the man's black hair and beard, sparkled with specks of snow and fragments of window glass.

The darkness inside the Jaguar prevented him seeing an abrasion on the man's face or noticing mud and grass stains on the disarranged clothing. Although he had been shot three times, at close range, the wounds were clustered around the head and torso rather than the lower limbs. He saw no blood and told us he got none on his hands when he touched the corpse.

Tom then made, what would later prove to be, a crucial observation. Both the dead man's legs lay along on the seat, the right bent and the left straight. A police photograph, taken a few hours later (see above) shows the legs curled side-by-side on the seat. An apparently trivial observation this would prove to be of crucial importance to the defence. The lower part of the man's left trouser leg was pulled up, exposing a few inches of bare flesh. Tom reached down and closed his fingers around the calf in an attempt to shake him awake. As he did so he thought how incongruously thin it was for such a large man. 'Hey, mate,' he said loudly, 'you can't park here!'

There was no response. The flesh was cold under his touch, and Tom realised he was dealing with a corpse. 'Hey, mate,' he muttered. 'You've had it!'

Former regular soldier Tom Leak had seen many corpses before and was neither scared nor upset by his discovery. Closing the car door, he turned back up the A182 and walked quickly to the nearest phone box, about two hundred yards away on the opposite side of the road outside South Hetton post office. On his way, he met his three friends who had left the mine later than usual. Tom told them about finding the body, explained he was going to call the police and suggested someone went to the nearby police house to rouse the local constable. While Len Ellis went to do this, Billy Jones and John Leslie Marshall walked to the Mark X.

Marshall, a colliery supervisor with first aid training, opened the door and felt the dead man's leg without, he testified in court, altering its position. Walking around to the vehicle's off-side, he discovered that the rear window had been shot out. Reaching in through the opening he felt for a pulse in the neck. There was none. The driver's window was wound down and Marshall again put his hand into the car to try and switch on some lights. He later testified to depressing two switches on the dashboard, without effect, before returning them to their original positions. He found that the ignition was still switched on, the key hanging in place, and turned it off. The men then noticed that the side lights were glowing faintly and the wipers, in a partly raised position, weren't working.

Tom Leak, meanwhile, had dialled 999 and the operator connected him to Peterlee police station, some four miles away.

'There's a body under the bridge,' he told the PC who answered.

'Where's that then?'

'Pesspool Bridge. It's the first bridge you come to in South Hetton.'

'Oh, is that what they call it? Right, we'll send a car. It'll be along in a couple of minutes.'

Tom returned to the vehicle at almost the same moment as the hastily dressed local PC, Maurice Cluer. On examining the body, Cluer reported seeing blood dripping from the wounds. As with the miner's description of Sibbet's right leg dangling in the seat well, this finding should have proved hugely significant when it came to estimating time of death. In the event, because they conflicted with the prosecution case, Leak's observation was dismissed and Cluer's report suppressed.

Shortly after 5.30 am, an Austin Westminster, driven by PCs James Grierson and Michael Dominic Hafferty, pulled up by the bridge. The two officers had been on duty, between 10 pm and 6 am, that night. Shortly before midnight they had driven along the A182 and under Pesspool Bridge. This would have been around the time when, according to the police theory, the murder must have been taking place at a point not far down the road. Neither of them had seen or heard anything out of the usual.

Robbery had not been the motive. Police found £146 3s. 6d stuffed into his right hip pocket, his wallet was still in his jacket and there was an expensive watch on his wrist. The police quickly identified the dead man as 33-year-old Angus Stuart Sibbet. As an employee of Newcastle's leading entertainment company, Social Club Services, his job had been to travel around local miners' clubs collecting money from hundreds of One-Armed Bandits the company had installed.

Sibbet, they later discovered, loved the high life. He drove a new and expensive car, lived in a fashionable Newcastle neighbourhood, gambled regularly, drank champagne and patronised the city's most exclusive nightclubs and restaurants. Although married with a young daughter, he supported two mistresses and was constantly weaving a web of subterfuge to keep the one who knew he was married from the other who did not. As we shall see, whether in his sexual or criminal exploits, he played for high stakes and was never afraid to take a chance.

Walking home from Pesspool Bridge in the dim pre-dawn, Tom Leak could have no idea of the tragic chain of events his 'moment of 'nosiness', as he described it to us, would trigger. Had anyone suggested he had stumbled across the victim of a gangland killing the no-nonsense Geordie miner would have laughed in their face.

'Murder?' he told us. 'I never thought it were murder - never in the world. Things like that don't happen in South Hetton.'

Chapter Two: Men From A Strange World

'This is to assure you, if you need assurance, that North Country hospitality is no legend where Newcastle is concerned.' City Guide, 1967

Eight weeks later, at 10.30, on the morning of March 6, 1967, Mr Justice Patrick Murphy O'Connor took his seat on one of the red-leather upholstered chairs in the 19th century splendour of Newcastle's Number One courtroom. He was about to start the eagerly anticipated trial of Michael Luvaglio and Dennis Stafford for the cold-blooded killing of Angus Stuart Sibbet.

Hours before the court opened the narrow, cobbled, streets around the Moot Hall, where the case was being tried, had been crowded with onlookers. The arrival, shortly after nine, of police cars carrying the accused from Durham Prison, caused such excitement that officers struggled to hold back the surging crowd. During the trial armed police patrolled streets around the court. Each of the ten men and two women on the jury was escorted to and from their homes and were kept under observation overnight. 'Precautions on such a scale have never been seen at any previous trial in the City,' a Regional Crime Squad officer told us.[1]

The Rise and Rise of Gangsters UK
Although the trials of London gangsters were still some months away, ripples made by this murky pool of ruthless professional criminals had already reached the North. There were rumours of Chicago-style racketeering, protection mobs and gang warfare. Whispers that anybody who stepped out of line would be swiftly and brutally dealt with. A Newcastle garage and three nightclubs had been gutted by fire after threatening phone calls. Newcastle, many feared, was fast becoming the 'Gangstertoon' of the North.

There was not only widespread fear of local gangsters but awareness of police investigations three hundred miles away in London. There a specially formed squad of murder squad detectives, led by Detective Chief Superintendent Leonard 'Nipper' Read was conducting operations which would soon lead to the arrest and conviction of both the notorious Richardson gang and the equally infamous Kray brothers Charles, Reginald and Ronald. It was a reflection too of the notoriety achieved by one of the accused, Dennis Stafford, whose criminal career, as we explain in Chapter Five, had been as colourful as it as it was widely publicised.

To better understand the likely attitude towards the accused we need to take a closer look at the social transformation the region had experienced in a few years.

[1] *Defence lawyers have long argued guarding a jury is hugely prejudicial. Research has shown the chances of acquittal with a guarded jury are much reduced. Jurors inevitably suspect that the accused must possess the resources to intimidate them. Furthermore, close contact between jurors and their police guards could be used to exert undue influence over them.*

Newcastle in a Time of Change
Many of those from the North-East who following the trial would have been old enough to remember the destitution caused some thirty years earlier by the closure of Palmer's Jarrow shipyard, engine works, blast furnaces and rolling mills. This cost the jobs of over 10,000 and left 70% of the local workforce unemployed. In 1936, widespread deprivation and desperation led to the famous Jarrow March on London by unemployed blue-collar workers. By the early 'sixties, prosperity had, to some extent, returned. But the relentless decline in the traditional industries of coal mining, steel smelting and ship building, made the future uncertain and kept wages low.

Within months of changes to the gaming laws, Newcastle had developed a night life second only to London in its vibrancy and popularity. Of the dozens of new nightclubs which opened, three played a significant role in our story. The Piccadilly Club owned by Michael Luvaglio and managed by Dennis Stafford; The Dolce Vita where Angus Sibbet enjoyed his last meal and from which he left to meet his killers and The Birdcage Club where he had arranged to meet up with Michael and Dennis.

One of Newcastle's most luxurious and lavishly equipped clubs, 'The Dolcey' had a cabaret lounge seating five hundred, an illuminated glass dance floor and a stage equipped with the latest in sound and lighting equipment. Major stars from Britain and America, who performed there included Tom Jones, Dean Martin, Jerry Lee Lewis, Ella Fitzgerald, The Hollies, Van Morrison and the Small Faces. The Beatles gave one of their earliest performances, outside Liverpool, at a Newcastle club for a fee of five shillings (25 pence). Many of the American artists were managed by Frank Sinatra's son, Frank Jnr and he, in turn, used London gangsters, the Kray twins, to take care of their security while in the UK.

These sophisticated nightspots were very different from the North-East's traditional working men's clubs. In place of smoked filled rooms with their drab décor, wooden seats, Newcastle Brown Ale and blue comedians, they offered elegant chairs and couches, upholstered in rich velvet. Rooms decorated with gold flock wallpaper and lit by crystal chandeliers. Food and drink served, on fine china and damask draped tables, by young, pretty and scantily dressed waitresses. Clubs offered gambling of all types. Roulette, blackjack, baccarat, poker tables and numerous fruit machines. Aptly named One Armed Bandits they promised punters the chance to win instant cash at the pull of a lever. While the rewards for those who played them was modest, they provided almost limitless wealth for those who owned them. Not always honestly.

The Police Investigate
After the murder trial, the police undertook a major enquiry into the gaming business. They soon established that players and the committees in

whose clubs they were installed, were being deprived of most of the machine's takings. But they had difficulty in proving who was getting what. Sometimes a single club steward was receiving the bribe on other occasions the whole club committee. To overcome this obstacle they prosecuted the companies, like Social Club Services, who had installed the machines. Usually on the basis that whilst they had claimed to provide new machines, they often delivered only reconditioned ones. In reality, club stewards could not have cared less. We spoke to many who said they would have been happy with cardboard boxes as long as they took plenty of money.

We found widespread resentment among, especially older blue-collar workers, towards the slick young men from London in their expensive suits, who ran the clubs, organised the gambling and owned the One-Armed Bandits. Men with soft hands, fast cars and seemingly limitless amounts of cash. Men who earned their money with none of the backbreaking labour necessary to provide the hard-earned coins gobbled up by their machines. *The Newcastle Journal* summed up their general mood in an article headlined: 'Men from a Strange World'. It was an accurate description of the way many in Newcastle felt about the accused.

The Murder Trial Starts

From the first hearings, Sibbet's murder attracted an enormous amount of press and public interest. People queued for hours to get a seat in the Magistrates' Court and when the full trial began, the Moot Hall's Number One court was filled to capacity. Long wooden benches in public galleries were packed with people eager to witness what was expected to be the most sensational trial in the City's history. The press box, on the judge's right, was filled by reporters from local and national papers. The well of the court bustled with police officers, solicitors and robed counsel. Leading for the Crown was Henry Scott, QC. while Rudolph Lyons, QC and Raymond Dean, QC. represented Dennis Stafford and Michael Luvaglio respectively.

Only the jury box, three benches stepped one above the other, presented rows of empty seats as the Clerk of Assize rose to his feet, and facing each of the accused in turn told them: 'You are charged on this indictment with murder, the particulars alleged being that you, on a day between the third day and the sixth day of January 1967, in the County of Durham, murdered Angus Stuart Sibbet. How say you ... are you Guilty or Not Guilty?'

Both pleaded not guilty and the jury was sworn. The defence exercised their right to object to prospective jurors only once, rejecting a man with a hearing aid. One juryman refused to take the oath on religious grounds and affirmed instead.

Before we study the evidence which the court heard during the five-day trial, it will be as well to look at a basic tenet of British justice. Juries, except under certain clearly defined circumstances, should remain in ignorance of any previous criminal record which the accused may have. The law has since changed in some respects. The general exceptions being if defence counsel attacks the character of a prosecution witness or attempts to paint their client as an honest, upright citizen, when the opposite is true.

While neither of these happened during the trial of Dennis Stafford and Michael Luvaglio, it seems highly likely the jury were aware of Stafford's past life, which, as we have mentioned, had been widely publicised. On several occasions he had made front-page headlines in the national press, and even more frequently in the local papers of the North-East.

With the jury selected the trial could start. Over the next two weeks, the court was to hear a mish mash of evidence, some of it fabricated, often conflicting and sometimes contradictory. It was to become a case that would, for over half a century puzzle, would puzzle and frustrate all who studied. It was also destined to become and, still remains, a stain on British justice and a prime example of how not to conduct a murder investigation.

Before we examine the details of this extraordinary trial, let's take a closer look at the defendants themselves.

Who were Michael Luvaglio and Dennis Stafford and how did they end up spending over a decade behind bars for a murder they simply could not have committed?

Chapter Three: The Luvaglio Brothers

'Alas regardless of their fate,
The little victims play.
No thoughts have they of ills to come,
Or cares beyond today'. Thomas Gray

The Luvaglio brothers were born a few years before the outbreak of the Second World War, Vincent in 1932 and Michael in 1937. Their father Francis, a third-generation Italian immigrant, was a successful and prosperous Master Tailor, who headed the tailoring department in London's fashionable Army and Navy Stores

Their childhood was a happy one, spent mostly in the leafy West London suburb of Mitcham, not far from Wimbledon. Michael loved animals and had three dogs, a German shepherd, spaniel and a collie which he walked every evening on his return from school.

In 1940, their father Francis was called up for military service and in April 1941, the neighbourhood was heavily bombed with considerable loss of life. One of Michael's most vivid early memories is finding half a human head in their back garden following one such raid. To ensure their safety, the brothers were sent to live with a relative in the comparative safety of the Berkshire market town of Newbury. At the local school Michael was badly bullied on account of a pronounced stammer. He looked to his older brother, in the same school but two classes higher, for protection. 'Vince was like a god to me,' Michael recalls. 'Always looking after his little brother.'

The Making of an Entrepreneur

From an early age Vince was also looking out for ways to make money. Not always honestly. At nine, he organised a gang of local boys to raid orchards for apples. In wartime Britain such fresh fruit was in very scarce supply. He sold them to local green grocers and shared the money with other gang members. As mastermind Vince naturally held on to the lion's share.

Another money-making scheme was to dress five-year-old Michael in a tattered shirt and torn shorts, smear his face with grime and get him to stand outside the large American air force base. Unable to resist the pleas of what they believed to be a pathetic, half-starved, street kid, the GI's lavished these treats such as chocolates and cigarettes on him. Michael would have this booty onto his brother who sold them to local newsagents. As usual, most of the cash ended up in Vince's pocket.

Michael - Mathematician and Musician

A talented boy, Michael was especially good at maths. This helped him pass his 11- plus exam with flying colours and was awarded as place at the prestigious St John Fisher School in Purley, South London. This is a still flourishing school whose prospectus lists its chief aim as turning out 'Young

Catholic Gentlemen'.

Michael attended as a dayboy, but the school also took boarders. While these were not allowed to buy comics, dayboys were allowed to do so. On learning this Vincent, who had just started his National Service with the RAF Military Police, spotted a marketing opportunity. He instructed his brother buy comics and resell them, at a generous mark-up, to his less privileged fellow pupils. It was a pattern of behaviour that was to continue into adulthood.

Entrepreneur Vincent would spot a demand. His bright and obedient younger brother would take the risks and be grateful for any rewards his older brother sent his way.

Called up to do National Service in 1957, Vince joined the RAF Military Police and spent some months as a prison guard. On one occasion, he told his horrified younger brother, he ordered the prisoners to scrub clean a landing using toothbrushes. He considered this an amusing anecdote then, seeing the shocked look on his brother's face, added hastily. 'Only joking of course.' But Michael was fairly certain he was not.

Vince was a tough-minded young man well able to look after himself. In this he was very different from his gentle younger brother who went out of his way to avoid confrontations. He was, in the words of Dennis Stafford, 'the last person you'd want at your side in a fight. Even a pillow fight!'

In addition to his skill with numbers, Michael played both violin and piano to a professional level. As a young man he performed at Humphrey Lyttleton's Oxford Street jazz club and recorded a version of Bad Penny Blues with the great trumpeter himself.

Called up for his National Service, in 1955, Michael also joined the RAF as an aircraft loader. This is a complex, extremely responsible job, involving calculating the weight of cargo and passengers to ensure each aircraft is correctly balanced. A miscalculation on his part could have ended in disaster for all on board.

During the Suez invasion, in November 1956, he was flown out to Egypt with the 16th Parachute Brigade. Due to a communications confusion he was forced to jump out of the plane alongside them. Never having been taught how to parachute he broke his leg badly on landing and was flown home to the UK. Discharged a few months later, he was offered a similar job with a civil airline. Instead he chose to work as an accountant, first for a London printing firm and then at Trusthouse Forte.

Working for the Krays

On leaving the RAF, in 1953, Vince took a job as a salesman in a TV shop whose owner was friends with his father. Within months he had left to work with the Kray Twins, managing their Soho gambling business. In 1954, realising he could make more money working for himself than for the Krays, Vincent set up in business for himself. He started by selling second-hand televisions, radios and records all of which were in great demand. Later he obtained a UK wide franchise for a television converter which enabled TV sets only able to pick up BBC programmes to receive ITV as well.

His business prospered to such an extent he invited his financially astute brother to join the firm. Michael's first job involved installing the converters and adjusting the X-shaped aerials needed to pick up ITV signals. Often this involved hanging out of upstairs windows while Angus Sibbet, who had also recently joined the firm, held him by the legs. On one occasion, when Angus was off sick, Vincent took over and accidently let go of his brother as he was hanging upside down twenty feet above the ground. Michael fell and broke his leg for a second time.

The Luvaglios and Angus Sibbet

Vincent and Michael first met Sibbet in 1957 when they became regulars at a Chinese restaurant, near their offices, which Angus helped run. The three became friends and, few months later, when the restaurant failed, Vince offered him a job. By this time, Landa had moved from old televisions to importing Wurlitzer jukeboxes, pin tables and espresso machine. These he and his brother rented to the increasing numbers of popular coffee bars. Although, until the passing of the 1960 Gambling Act, Fruit Machines were illegal, he also began bringing in reconditioned One-Armed Bandits from America.

'We had machines in at least ten coffee bars in and around London, including Mayfair, and subsequently further afield,' Michael recalls. 'We had them on both Brighton and Blackpool Piers and, after 1960, in Brighton's newly opened casino.'

As his business expanded, Vince developed close, and corrupt, relationships with police officers. These helped his stay one step ahead of the law. On one occasion, warned of an impending raid on the Brighton pier amusement arcade, Vincent ordered his local manager to toss all the fruit machines into the sea. The police who swarmed onto the pier, left empty handed. The story illustrates Vince's willingness to corrupt those in authority and the ruthlessness with which he safeguarded his business interests.

The Law is Changed

Before 1961 all off-course betting, from bingo to bookmaking and card games to casinos, was illegal in the UK. Restrictive and outdated laws meant that even placing a small wager on a game of bridge could land you in trouble. With no high street betting shops, punters could only enjoy a flutter either at the races or by telephoning a bookmaker. As a result, a vast network of illegal bookmakers, mostly under the control of criminal gangs, flourished.

After the Betting and Gaming Act became law, on January 1 1961, the true extent of Britain's appetite for gambling become apparent. From the first of March onwards applications poured into the Licensing Authorities to open betting shops. Within six months, 10,000 new premises had opened, and hundreds were applying for a licence every week. Other places where people could gamble, from humble high street Bingo Halls to lavishly decorated casinos, also expanded rapidly. Within five years of the Act being passed, over a thousand had opened their doors.

The Krays Move In

By the late 'fifties, the Luvaglios' coffee bar and gambling enterprises had expanded throughout London and across the South East. Business was booming and both brothers were making a great deal of money. But their success came at an increasing threat from London gangsters. Based in Bethnal Green, north of the Thames was 'The Firm' were headed by twins Ronnie and Reggie Kray with their older brother Charlie. The Kray's main source of income came from the 'insurance' they offered to clubs, bars, casinos and small businesses. Failure to purchase it resulted in premises being burned out or wrecked, staff intimidated, assaulted or in some instances murdered.

London south of the river was controlled by Charlie, Alan and Eddie Richardson. Based at a Greenwich scrap yard, KWP Metals, they were even more violent and sadistic than the Krays. Gang members included, George Cornell, later shot dead by Ronnie Kray, and 'Mad' Frankie Fraser. Known as the 'Torture Gang' they specialised in pulling out teeth, slicing off toes with a bolt cutter and impaling victims to the floor using 6-inch nails.

The Krays and the Richardsons were not the only gangsters operating out of London at the start of the 'swinging sixties.' The prospect of easy money, from both legal and illicit gambling attracted major criminals from Europe and the USA. In 1959 Tony 'Ducks' Carolla, who headed New York's Genovese Crime Family, sent one of his foot soldiers, David 'Gabe' Forman to England. His job was to open up the market for one-armed bandits previously used in the State of Maryland. A flamboyant individual, Forman started 'Las Vegas Coin Ltd' in London's Poland Street. Among those who worked for him, delivering fruit machines was 'Mad' Frankie Fraser from the Richardson gang. Ronnie and Reggie noted Vince's increasing success with growing resentment. On one occasion, Reggie accused Vincent of installing his own fruit-machines into their own clubs and beat him up as a punishment. Rather than establish their own business in competition, the Twins saw a far faster and cheaper way to dominate the lucrative gaming industry. By forcing the Luvaglios out of London.

One sunny July morning in 1960, Michael was alone at home when there was a knock on the door. He vividly remembers what happened next: 'There was this bloke with bowler hat, black jacket and striped trousers like a solicitor would wear and carrying a smart leather briefcase. He asked if I was Michael Luvaglio, and when I said I was, he opened his briefcase and took out a cutthroat razor. Placing the blade just under the knot of my tie he sliced it'.

The Rise and Fall of T. Dan Smith

A fish, they say, rots from the head. When it came to 'sixties Newcastle the rot started at the top of the City Council which, as the poet Phillip Larkin put it, was ruled 'By a cast of crooks and tarts.' The most powerful of these was Thomas Daniel Smith, better known as T. Dan Smith, who led Newcastle City Council, between 1960 and 1965. Nicknamed 'Mr Newcastle' and the 'Mouth of the Tyne' he was considered by many in politics as 'the most charismatic leader the North-East has ever produced'. A prominent figure in the Labour Party, his ambition was to transform the City into the 'Brasília of the North'. This would involve not just clearing slums, but demolishing rows of elegant Victorian buildings and replacing them with blocks of steel and concrete.

He had joined the Labour Party, aged eighteen, and risen swiftly through their ranks. When the Party took control of Newcastle, after winning the 1958 local elections, Smith was appointed Chairman of the Housing Committee and Leader of the City Council. His influence increased still further when he became chairman of the Northern Economic Planning Council. Through his public relations company, Dan developed a close association with London architect John Poulson. In return for bribes he awarded Poulson commissions worth several million pounds in today's money. This required him not only to act dishonestly himself but to encourage those around him to do the same. He created, in the words of one official: 'A fifth column of corrupt councillors to work for John Poulson.'

One of his closest allies on the council, was Alderman Andrew 'Andy' Cunningham. The autocratic, 55-year-old, Regional Secretary of the powerful General and Municipal Workers Union, he was also Chairman of the Durham Police Authority. Cunningham was, if anything, more corrupt than his boss. When jailing him for six years, in 1974, Mr Justice Waller summed up the Alderman's appetite for easy cash by remarking: 'You not only accepted money…you demanded it.'

Over the next few years, Smith personally pocketed some three and a half million pounds in today's money. His decorating company also prospered greatly, receiving more than half of the contracts for council housing. The boy who had grown up in a slum now enjoyed a lavish lifestyle. He drove a new Jaguar, licence plate DAN 68, educated his children at expensive private schools and bought a flat in London's exclusive St James. Using his newfound wealth and political clout, he assiduously cultivated senior Ministers in Harold Wilson's Labour Party. Among them were Deputy Prime Minister Edward Short, MP for Newcastle Central and Foreign Secretary George Brown.

Landa's Network of Corruption

From his first days in Newcastle, Vince Landa worked hard to develop a close relationship with both Smith and Cunningham. He fully appreciated not only the benefits they brought him but the trouble they could cause if he ever fell out with them. He was warned: 'Whatever you do don't upset Andy. He's a dangerous man when he wants to be. Even Cabinet Ministers are frightened of him.'

If T. Dan Smith wanted a favour, Landa would bend over backwards to help. In June 1964, for example Poulson asked 'Mr Newcastle' to book accommodation in a luxury Spanish hotel. He wanted to provide a free holiday for an anonymous VIP guest and his wife. Smith asked Landa to make the arrangements. Vince, who owned a hotel in Palma and knew the island well, booked a private villa in the grounds of Majorca's five-star Formentor Royal Hideaway Hotel in the name of T. Dan Smith. He later learned the VIP had been Foreign Secretary George Brown and his wife Sophie. This knowledge Vince carefully stored away for possible future use should he need a political favour from one of the highest in the land.

Fast Track to Fortune

Within three years of arriving in Newcastle, the Luvaglio brothers had installed one-armed bandits in clubs from Yorkshire to Edinburgh. While Social Club Services was opening nightclubs, organising wrestling bouts and managing bingo halls, its chief business was servicing the needs of the North-East's hundreds of working men's clubs. Legally they were only allowed to install two One-Armed Bandits in each club, but because the law also permitted two backup machines, each could be provided with four. Two were located in the main club room with one each in the gents and ladies' lavatories. These were not supposed to be used and had, by law, to be covered with a cloth. In reality, the machine in the ladies took more money than the two in the bar itself. Wives were gambling the wages handed to them by their husbands, in the hope of winning enough money to feed their family.

What club members never knew was that only a small proportion of their hard-earned sixpences, which fed the machines, was ever returned to them. Vince and Michael received 60% of whatever money was collected, 20% paid off committee members and 20% was left in the machines to pay out winnings. All this cash was collected, twice a week, by Angus Sibbet. The three held regular business meetings and saw each other socially about once a week, usually for dinner at La Dolce Vita. 'Our relationship was absolutely harmonious,' Michael insists. 'I was very fond of Angus and never had the slightest reason to think Vince wished him any harm. We were all doing incredibly well.'

Michael paid cash for an Edwardian house in Chelsea Grove where he lived with his girlfriend Pat Burgess. He also bought numerous buy-to-let properties in and around Newcastle and, in March 1965, opened The Piccadilly Club above a garage on Bath Lane in the City centre.

He invested £65,000 (over £1 million today) fitting out the club which had three bars, a dining and dancing area and gaming rooms offering everything from roulette to blackjack. In June 1966 Vince took a dislike to the manager Michael had appointed and replaced him with Londoner, Dennis Fielding. Fielding, who had previously managed a successful club in Soho had been recommended to Vince by his friend Reader Harris.[1]

It was not until many months later that Michael was told Dennis Fielding was in fact Dennis Stafford, a career criminal whose extraordinary story we will describe in Chapter Five. Stafford's main job was to run the club, but he quickly became involved in booking cabaret acts, using his girlfriend Selena Jones as his show-business contact.

Among the world class stars he booked were Dean Martin, Tom Jones, Mel Torme, Adam Faith, Diana Dors and Dusty Springfield. For a few months business boomed as The Piccadilly Club rapidly grew in popularity and it seemed like his investment would pay handsomely. He could not have been more wrong.

The Krays Pay a Call
In June 1966 the Kray brothers visited Newcastle intending to meet Vincent. Learning in advance of their visit, Landa tipped off Jack Vinton, high ranking Newcastle police officer. When the Twins arrived, accompanied by several heavies, they were followed everywhere. Their attempts to force their way into the Piccadilly Club and confront Michael were thwarted by the two burly ex-miner doormen. Michael slipped out via a rear exit. They were, however, welcomed visitors to the Dolce Vita.

Their attempts to persuade Durham working men's clubs to take out their 'insurance' proved equally unsuccessful. In London it was relatively easy to threaten the individual owners and managers of nightclubs, bars and casinos. In Northumberland they found themselves up against a committee of a dozen miners who were unimpressed by bully boy tactics from 'soft Southerners' and told them so in no uncertain terms. Humiliated and furious the twins headed back to the safety of Bethnal Green. Ronnie, especially, was determined the time would soon come when these insults could be repaid and their reputations as the 'hardest men in Britain' restored.

Also receiving a humiliating rebuff from both club committee members and Vince Landa, was a notorious Scottish gangster Arthur Thompson known in Glasgow as the 'Godfather'. For more than thirty years he masterminded a wide

[1] *A wealthy barrister, businessman and long serving Tory MP for Heston and Isleworth. Reader Harris, was arrested in 1969, charged with carrying on company business with intent to defraud the company's creditors, falsifying the balance sheet, and deceiving investors as to the company's financial state. Although acquitted, his reputation was ruined as a result of his lengthy association with fraudulent businessmen and companies that went bankrupt. He was dismissed from his seat in Parliament and never again allowed to stand as a Conservation MP.*

range of criminal activities in Scotland and north of the border, including protection, robbery and, during the 'eighties, drugs during the so-called 'Ice Cream Wars.' We shall be taking a close look at this career criminal's involvement in Sibbet's murder in the penultimate chapter.

Arson at the Piccadilly Club
Michael's troubles started in mid-July, some six weeks after Ronnie and Reggie had been barred from his club. Fights broke out, equipment was vandalised, and threats made against the staff. Worse soon followed.
Around 3.30 in the afternoon of September 25, passers-by spotted smoke pouring from the club's first and second-floor windows. The alarm was sounded and a total of forty firemen and eight appliances fought one of the biggest blazes in the City's history. Despite their best efforts, the club was gutted with damage estimated, in today's money, at over a million pounds .
When the embers had cooled, detectives and forensic experts moved in to investigate the cause of the inferno. Petrol cans were found among the blackened debris and two men were reported running from the premises shortly before the fire started. Twenty detectives worked on the case for weeks, but no arrests were made.
At first the police suspected Michael and Vincent of starting the blaze for insurance purposes but dismissed this theory when told that after sprinklers had been installed, insurance cover had been greatly reduced. Furthermore, as Vince pointed out, the club had been turning over some £3,000 (£156,000 in today's money) a week and had just paid out £5,000 (£94,000) in gaming tax.
The Piccadilly Club blaze was not the Luvaglio's only property to be gutted by fire. The Quay Club and Pear Tree Garage, which Social Club Services also owned, were burned down under equally suspicious circumstances.
Vince told the Newcastle Journal about the threatening phone calls he had received, the demands for protection money and the fights that frightened away customers. The arson, violence and intimidation against the Luvaglio brothers' business empire were a reflection of increasing gang warfare. Although the City's corruption and criminality had benefited Vince when he first arrived in the North East, it now seemed determined to destroy him.

Landa Lord of the Manor
In early 1963, Vince, Gwen and their six children, left their modest Peterlee council house for the baronial splendour of Dryderdale Hall. ₁ The Grade II listed building, which cost him £1 million in today's money, had been built for a local banking family in 1872. The Hall stood in 130 acres of park and farmland, with two farms, an elegant gate lodge, woodlands and a lake. There were extensive garages for Vince's white Rolls Royce, Pontiac Grand Prix, Arcadian shooting brake, and red E-type Jaguar.

Landa furnished his new home lavishly. The entrance hall was decorated with crystal chandeliers and a huge stuffed peacock. Bedrooms on the upper floors were reached via an electric lift. In an octagonal tower, next to his first-floor bedroom, Vince installed an astronomical telescope. The darkly panelled dining room had a banqueting table seating twenty. In the drawing room were two long, curved, sofas upholstered in gold velvet, each capable of seating sixteen. The walls were hung with souvenirs from around the world. Exotically painted masks from Mexico, bongo drums from Africa, carved elephants from India, wooden gods from the Pacific, daggers and bullfighting banderillos from Spain.

Gwen explained to guests these had been collected during their frequent holidays abroad. 'We have been everywhere but South America and Russia,' she told one visitor. 'Over Easter we all enjoyed a holiday in the West Indies and are planning to take our six children to Australia after Christmas.'

Perhaps the Hall's most notable and, in the early 'sixties, less usual feature was the large number of CCTV cameras and television sets in different parts of the house. Further security was provided by three large German shepherd guard dogs.

While he had become extremely wealthy in a short time, Vince was acutely aware of the growing threats this success had created for his rapidly expanding empire, himself and his family. Like any canny businessman he decided to keep his friends close and his enemies even closer.

Vince Landa - Lavish Host & Generous Businessman

Within weeks of Landa moving in, Dryderdale became known for its sumptuous parties and dinners to which the cream of Newcastle society was invited. T. Dan Smith and Andrew Cunningham were regular guests. Among other influential citizens quaffing champagne and nibbling canapes were Aldermen and Councillors, local officials, Union leaders, Labour Party politicians, nightclub owners and senior police officers.

The nature of Vince's relationship with the Durham police is illustrated by an occasion when he was driving a business associate around Sunderland in his new Buick convertible. Not finding anywhere to park, he abandoned the huge car in the middle of a busy street. Snapping his finger at a passing constable he curtly instructed the officer to keep an eye on his vehicle while they were away. Coming to attention and giving him a smart salute, the policeman said: 'It will be my honour Mr. Landa.'

---

[1] *When the gangster film Get Carter, staring Michael Caine and Britt Ekland was shot in 1971, Dryderdale Hall was chosen as the home of the chief villain, shady businessman Cliff Brumby who had controlling interests in local amusement arcades. The film was based on the book Jack's Return Home by Ted Lewis and was heavily influenced by Sibbet's murder.*

It wasn't only the rich and powerful who benefited from Vincent's generosity. Landa changed miner Ray Thubron's life in the early 'sixties when he made him his right-hand man. 'We went daft', he told us frankly. 'We drove big American cars. I used to park by outside my council house in Silksworth. We had endless parties; all expenses paid trips to London. Each year all his employees could enjoy a free two weeks holiday at his luxury hotel in Majorca. Every petty crook in the area wanted to work for Mr Big – Vince Landa. Vince was big all right – and getting bigger every day.'

He also went out of his way to develop a reputation as a generous boss and charitable business leader. When Dickie Richman, one of Social Club Services' senior managers – the employee who helped thwart a police raid on Brighton Pier a few years earlier – developed kidney disease, Vince came to his aid. He imported one of the first dialysis machines from America and donated it to Newcastle hospital. Later he purchased and gave away several more kidney machines and distributed them to other hospitals in the area.

The Luvaglios Make the Big Time

By the end of 1966 Vince and Michael had become two of the wealthiest and most powerful men in the North East. In early January 1966, Vince proposed launching Social Club Services on the London Stock Exchange with the support of several high-ranking politicians, including Lord Boothby, Conservative Home Secretary Reginald Maudling, Edward Short and George Brown. The 49% of the shares the Luvaglios' proposed to sell were valued at £8 million, around £135 million in today's money.

On December 20, with the Public Offering only weeks away, Vince and his family, accompanied by Michael, Pat Burgess and Dennis Stafford flew to Majorca to spend Christmas at their hotel. Before leaving, Michael gave his best friend Angus a brand-new Mark X as a Christmas present. It was in this vehicle that Sibbet's bullet ridden body would be found only a couple of weeks later.

As the jet lifted off from Newcastle airport, Vincent and Michael must have believed their boyhood dreams of becoming vastly wealthy were about to come true. Vince was also confident powerful friends in politics and the police had made him untouchable by either his enemies or the law. In both these beliefs they could not have been more wrong.

Chapter Four: The Life and Death of a Gambling Man

'For some reason his presence on this earth was not desirable, so he was killed.' Mr Henry Scott, Q.C.

Around 11.15 on the night of 4 January 1967, freelance photographer Tom Oxley pushed open one of the wooden-slatted doors of La Dolce Vita nightclub, on Newcastle's Low Friars Street and stepped inside. A few weeks earlier he had taken pictures of Angus Sibbet at a party and one of his reasons for visiting the club that night was to collect the money he was owed for prints. Oxley arrived just as Angus was leaving. After a brief conversation, Sibbet took out his wallet and settled the account.

'I was just in time getting the bill paid,' Oxley told us with a grim smile.

Apart from the killers, the photographer is the last known person to have seen the bearded, man alive.

A Small Time Crook Who Made the Big Time

Angus Stuart Sibbet was born in Newcastle on 2 July 1934. His childhood ambition was to follow his father and uncle into the army. At eighteen-months he contracted polio and, despite numerous operations, was left with a permanent limp. On leaving school, at sixteen, he worked in a shoe shop while waiting impatiently for his eighteenth birthday and the start of his National Service. To his dismay he was rejected due to his weakened left leg. Refusing to accept the army's decision, Angus spent months bombarding them with letters demanding a more detailed medical examination. Impressed by his keenness, they finally agreed and this time he was passed fit. At the end of 1952, aged eighteen years and six months, he became a National Serviceman.

Angus Goes to War

The Korean war, which started in June 1950, offered him a chance to prove himself in action. In order to get to the front line, he signed on as a regular soldier, serving in Korea and the Middle East. After serving four years he left the army and settled in London. In 1957, with his brother James and two partners, he opened a Chinese restaurant in South London. As we mentioned in the previous chapter, it was there he had first met Vince and Michael. The three became close friends and when he married, on 25 January 1957, Michael was his best man and Vincent gave the happy couple an expensive wedding gift.

When the restaurant began struggling financially, Vince offered Angus a job with his fast-growing firm. 'He was a good lad up till then,' his father told us. 'But he fell into bad company. I went to see him once or twice, and he was mixed up with some unsavoury characters.'

One of Vince's South London coffee bars was next door to a jeweller which Angus and two of his friends decided to burgle. The raid was successful, but Sibbet was arrested while attempting to fence the stolen goods.

He was sentenced to two years' imprisonment. Released in late 1958 he returned to work for Landa. When, in 1959, his father became seriously ill, his friend and generous employer offered to drive him home to Newcastle.

Angus Lives the High Life
Working for the Social Club Services made Angus wealthy. When he co-founded the company, Vince Landa gave him 49% of the shares. Later, after Michael Luvaglio became a director, his shareholding was split between the two of them. Even so, this meant that, when the company was about to go public, in 1967, he stood to make millions out of the deal. This, as we shall see in this chapter, was never enough for him. Greedy, self-centred and dishonest he was determined to grab even more of the company, even if this meant cheating his long-term friend and business partner Vince.

Within a year of the start-up, he was able to buy a three storey, detached house in Dunston where he lived with his wife Brenda and eight year-old daughter Karen, naming his new home 'Hi-De-Hi' and converted one of the downstairs rooms into a bar, complete with public-house style counter. It was here that he entertained his celebrity friends, who included Tom Jones and Engelbert Humperdinck.

Apart from his luxuriously furnished Dunston house, Angus funded a second home, in St George's Terrace, for his mistress Doreen Hall. Unknown to Doreen, Angus also paid for the upkeep of his second mistress, Doreen's sister Joyce, who lived a few miles away in Gateshead. While Joyce knew he was carrying on with her sister, Doreen remained in the dark about the situation. To maintain this complicated relationship and ensure his wife remained ignorant of both his mistresses, Angus would send himself postcards summoning him to fictitious business meetings. When phoning to put off a rendezvous with one sister in order to meet the other, he always public callbox rather than a nightclub, to avoid the music being heard.

His success in managing this complicated arrangement can be judged by an exchange at the trial. Sibbet's monosyllabic chauffeur and bodyguard Albert Ginley was being was cross-examined by Rudolph Lyons QC, for the defence.

'Did he [Angus Sibbet] live with his wife?' Lyons asked.
'No.'
'He lived with Doreen Hall, did he not?'
'Yes.'
'And that was at St George's Terrace, Newcastle?'
'Yes'.
'And that is where you lived?'
'Yes'.

'And although he was living with Doreen, he was having an affair for a very long time with Doreen's sister Joyce?'
'Yes'.
'And she lived at 38 St Edmund's Road in Gateshead?'
'Yes'.
'Is it correct that he was always making excuses to Doreen, false excuses to Doreen to cover up his association with Joyce, her sister?'
'Yes.'
'You have been at both houses frequently, of course?'
'Yes'.
'You lived in one of them. Is this the position, that Joyce knew about Doreen, with whom he was living more or less permanently, but Mr Sibbet tried to keep from Doreen his association with Joyce?'
'Yes'.
'Did Mr Sibbet often tell you how he used to leave the Dolce Vita in order to meet Joyce?'
'Yes'.

Sibbet's Unconventional Sex Life

Angus' love life was as unconventional as it was complex. He photographed and taped himself having sex with the sisters, games which often involved an unusual use for bananas and cucumbers. His sexual appetite was equalled only by his gluttony. The best tables were reserved for him at top Newcastle restaurants and night clubs, where he surrounded himself with people, often total strangers. These he would wine and dine lavishly at his own expense. He wore expensive suits, sported a gold watch, carried hundreds of pounds in his wallet and drove luxury cars. The impression he liked to give was of a high-flying executive in the gaming industry. In fact, his job was menial, and his wages moderate. How then did he manage to accumulate so much money in such a short time?

The wealth of this one time £5 a week shoe salesman was partly due to the way in which Vince structured his fruit-machine empire, as we described in the previous chapter. But he also took cash from the machines without Landa's knowledge as well as stealing from one-armed bandits owned by other companies.

We heard reports of cars laden with cash collected from the machines being stolen from outside the clubs. We cannot say for certain whether Sibbet, with his previous conviction for theft, was responsible for any of these. What we do know is that in the pocket of his smartly tailored suit Angus carried a passport to instant cash. Keys with which he could unlock any fruit machine in Durham. 'Whenever Angus turned up our takings went down,' a club owner told us sadly.

Landa Accuses Sibbet

Soon after the trial, when Social Club Services collapsed into bankruptcy, Landa fled abroad with his wife and six children to escape arrest on fraud charges. He was to remain abroad for the next thirteen years, living in Majorca, Italy and Sicily. In August 1967, as part of their investigations into corruption in the fruit-machine industry, he was interviewed in Majorca by two reporters from the People newspaper. Vince admitted introducing a system whereby club stewards were bribed to assist the smooth running of his business. A system whose cost rapidly spiralled out of control. By 1967, he estimated that more than £3 million a year (in today's money) was going straight into the pockets of club officials and employees. Sibbet, he claimed, was the worst offender, stealing £1,600 (nearly £30,00 in today's money) a week from his own and other people's machines. He told the journalists he had once employed a private detective to see how Sibbet was spending so much money. Was it wine, women or song? The detective told him it was all three!

In fact, the only vice in which Angus Sibbet never indulged was smoking to which he was strongly opposed. He even objected to passengers smoking in his car. Which makes a discovery the police made in the Mark X, and then kept from the defence, even more surprising and potentially incriminating, as we will explain in Chapter Seven.

Mechanical Money Trees

In making these accusations, Landa was being more than a little economical with the truth. While Angus certainly helped himself to considerable sums of money each week from the machines owned by Social Club Services, he did so largely with Vince's consent and connivance.

Because his company rented machines to clubs on a percentage basis (a practice which later became illegal), it was important both for the club and the company that equipment was in constant use. For this they depended on the cooperation of the club stewards, who received no benefit when the machines were working properly. Indeed, this only added to their workload. Clubs became more crowded and customers were constantly demanding supplies of sixpences (2.5p in today's currency) with which to play the machines. This meant that when they broke down, as they inevitably did, the stewards had no incentive to get them repaired promptly. Realising the amount this was costing his business, Vince decided to offer stewards a suitable incentive in the shape of a 20% cash bonus every time a machine was emptied.

Officially this happened once a fortnight, but in the week between official openings, Sibbet would extract up to £50, splitting the money with the steward. At one club, a forty-one-year-old steward told us how he accepted payments from Sibbet in exchange for letting him steal from machines on hire from Social Club Services. Nine months before his death the steward we talked to claimed he discontinued the arrangement, though he still received hand-outs from other collectors he allowed to raid his machines.

Sibbet also discovered the internal counters, which recorded the number of jackpots paid out, on some of the older machines could be tripped using nothing more sophisticated than a screwdriver. This registered a false jackpot and the money, up to £5, was split between himself and the club stewards. When entertaining at a night club Sibbet would often leave his guests, at around midnight, returning an hour or so later with more than enough money to settle the bill. As a friend told us, 'It were just like nipping out to the bank.' We were told how it was not uncommon for him to drive around with his car boot filled to overflowing with bags stuffed with coins.

On the face of it there seems no good reason why Landa should have levelled such an accusation against his murdered employee since, by doing so, he provided a motive for himself being behind the killing. A likely explanation is that, at the time of the interview, Vince Landa was on the run from the UK police and fighting extradition back to Britain and may have wanted to appear the victim of a corrupt employee rather than the prime mover of that dishonesty. Although he never mentioned it to the reporters, Landa had another reason for feeling aggrieved with Sibbet and it concerned his killing of a pedestrian.

The Death of Vera Stamp

In early 1961, while driving at speed through the coastal village of Ryehope, Vince had accidentally knocked down and killed 59-year-old Vera Stamp. Instead of stopping, he fled the scene. Although the police never traced the hit-and-run driver, his identity became known to Angus Sibbet who stored it away for future use. Four years later, when Vince and his family were on holiday abroad, Angus decided the moment had come to use it. He forged a letter, purporting to have come from the Durham police and mailed it to Social Club Services. In it he stated they had tracked down the driver and wanted to interview him, under caution, on his return. The idea was to scare Landa into remaining abroad, so smoothing Sibbet's path to a takeover of the company. After the letter had been read out to him over the phone, Vince got in touch with a well-placed contact in the Newcastle police who assured him it was a hoax.

Sibbet Fears for His Life

While always ready to take risks, in both his personal and working life, Angus was also a cautious man. He knew Reggie and Ronnie Kray had visited La Dolce Vita, a few weeks earlier and that like himself, they were eager to muscle in on Landa's lucrative empire. He was also uncomfortably aware that one of the men behind the other one-armed bandits he was emptying might decide to teach him a lesson. Quite likely a permanent one. In addition to going almost everywhere with his chauffeur and minder, the tall and muscular Albert Ginley, he frequently hired a tough ex-boxer, Paddy Hallettt, to accompany him on his rounds. Since he was Irish, Angus typically referred to the burly Hallett as

'Mick'. As we explain in a later chapter, this apparently trivial point was to assume considerable significance during the murder trial. On one occasion he was invited to meeting, late at night, on a disused airfield. In his world such arrangements were not unusual, and Angus initially agreed. Warned it would be attended by some men from London, however, he stayed well away.

Sibbet's Final Hours

Always a late riser, it was just after ten o'clock that Sibbet got out of bed to begin his last day on earth. He had spent the night with Doreen Hall at her home in St George's Terrace and left the house in a Ford Corsair driven by Albert Ginley. He was driven first to Social Club Services main office, a two-storey terraced block in Low Row, Sunderland, about twelve miles from Newcastle. Leaving Ginley in the car he went up to a first-floor office where he met Michael Luvaglio and Dennis Stafford, just back from their holiday in Majorca. He wanted to discuss some deals they had planned shortly before Christmas.

At the trial Michael explained: 'It was not only one particular deal, there was about six or seven different clubs where he said that definite sales, more or less, would be done. Of course, there was no contracts with them because I would have to go to a meeting to get the contract, but he felt there was six or seven sales that he could do, this was over the Christmas period. He said that he was a bit short of money prior to Christmas and he was given £200 on account of the sales that would be done over the coming period.'
'Anticipating sales that could be done, as he thought, over the Christmas period,' suggested his defence counsel Raymond Dean.
'This, may I add, was done as more of a friendly gesture,' Michael answered. 'My brother was away, and I had not his authority to give him the money but I had known, as I said, Mr Sibbet a very long time and I knew that if he told me these sales would be done, they would be done'.

One important deal Sibbet had in mind involved the Newcastle Transport Club which they hoped to refurnish, redecorate and equip with closed circuit television and a discotheque at a total cost of about £8,000 (£156,000 in today's money). Luvaglio had already been to one meeting at the club before Christmas and both were eager to get the deal sewn up.

At about 1.30, Ginley drove Sibbet, Stafford and Luvaglio to the accounts department of Social Club Services over the District Bank in John Street, Sunderland. They stayed for about three quarters of an hour and then, according to Michael, Angus suggested meeting up at the Birdcage Club that night. Michael said he would phone to confirm the arrangement later that afternoon. Ginley then drove the three men to the Wheatsheaf Service Station on the outskirts of Sunderland, where Stafford and Luvaglio were dropped off. All three, Ginley reported, seemed on the best of terms. Sibbet was in high spirits, laughing and cracking jokes. From the Wheatsheaf, Ginley took Sibbet to his wife's home in Mountside Gardens arriving at around three o'clock. On the journey he told Ginley that he was delighted that Michael was back from Majorca, because they had a deal to complete together involving the Transport Club in Newcastle.

At five o'clock Sibbet received a phone call from Michael confirming their meeting that night. Sometime between 5.30 and 6.30 he arrived at Joyce Hall's flat in Gateshead where Ginley was waiting. He remained there until shortly after seven o'clock when he instructed Ginley to drive him to the home of Doreen Hall. She was visiting her parents in Sunderland, but Sibbet wanted to wash, change and pick up the Mark X for his own use that night. He had given Ginley the night off to see his girlfriend. Sibbet drove the Jaguar back to Joyce's home, arriving shortly after nine. He and his mistress immediately set off for La Dolce Vita. They made a detour to Windy Nook Road, Gateshead, to pick up Joyce's friend Ann Euington, and arrived at La Dolce Vita around about 9.35.

Sibbet's Last Supper

For his last meal, Sibbet ordered turkey, brussels sprouts and roast potatoes, washed down by two glasses of Bacardi rum and Cokes. According to Joyce Hall's evidence he left the club about 10.55, but Tom Oxley has no doubt that, when he met Sibbet on the stairs, it was at least twenty minutes later. The photographer was not called to testify at the trial and only his written statement was presented:

'I know the Dolce Vita Club. I went there on Wednesday the fourth of January 1967. On arrival I saw Angus Sibbet. I met him just at the foot of the stairs on his way out of the club. I spoke to him. This was about 11.15 pm.'

When we spoke to him, Oxley confirmed the time and explained the two had chatted for several minutes before Sibbet paid for the prints and they parted. Even if his estimate of the time is not absolutely accurate, there remains a gap in the evidence about Sibbet's movements for a period of up to twenty minutes. Had whatever he did during this time any bearing on the fate which overtook him later that night? One might have thought that, in that small and crowded night club, he must have talked to a number of people. Yet no such individual was ever traced. The alternative is that he spoke to someone on the telephone. If so, it seems unlikely he called either Dennis or Michael who were still together at Westmorland Rise, Peterlee. They, and three other witnesses, insist that no phone call was received. Who then did Sibbet speak to and why did that individual not come forward at the trial?

This is just one of a several mysteries about the case which were never solved.

What we can say for certain is that, if Tom Oxley's evidence is to be believed and there is no reason to doubt it, soon after 11.15 Sibbet walked from the bright lights of the club into the freezing darkness of Low Friar Street. Six hours later Tom Leak found him shot dead in the back of his Mark X.

Sibbet's Funeral

On Wednesday 18 January, a long cortege escorting the flower bedecked coffin of Angus Stuart Sibbet, made the slow five miles journey from Mountside Gardens to the City cemetery. There were at least a hundred and fifty mourners, including night-club employees, friends from London's East End, show-business celebrities and plain-clothes detectives interested in identifying the many 'known faces' who turned up to pay their respects. There we so many mourners the chapel's doors were left open to allow those outside to hear the service.

The man who started his working life earning less than £500 a year died intestate leaving an estate valued at over a quarter of a million pounds today. Amongst the scores of floral tributes at his graveside was a wreath of red roses from his widow, another from his boss Vincent Francis Landa and a lavish bouquet of lilies, which we were told, came from Ronnie, Reggie and Charlie Kray. His closest friend was absent from the service, Michael Luvaglio, as was Dennis Stafford. Both were behind bars, having been charged by Kell with his murder.

Chapter Five: Dennis Stafford - The Playboy Crook

'They say I gave Dennis away by sending a cable. I don't believe it. I think Scotland Yard found out in some other way.' Eileen Cook

Dubbed 'London's Cheekiest Crook' by the press, career criminal and flamboyant playboy Dennis Stafford was born Dennis Siegenberg, in 1934, near London's Petticoat Lane market. The family changed their name to Stafford, soon after he was born, so as to sound less Jewish. The family moved to Stoke Newington, while he was a toddler, and then to a new housing estate at Hackney in North London. His father, Joe, was a successful bookmaker and the family were comfortably off. At school, teachers found Dennis bright and likeable. Fellow pupils remember him as a born leader, strong-willed and never afraid of standing up for himself. He wasn't good at team games, which he disliked, but enjoyed trips to the local pool and became a strong swimmer.

At the start of World War II, he was evacuated to Redruth in Cornwall while his father went into the Royal Army Service Corps and later served in a tank transporter company. It was nearly six years before they were reunited in Hackney. Even then, Joe saw little of his son. His work as a bookmaker meant he was frequently away from home attending race meetings. For months he only saw his son briefly, when he came upstairs to kiss him good night. This, combined with Joe's basically gentle nature, meant there was little discipline at home and Dennis was allowed to do as he liked. Only once did Joe lose his temper and start to hit the boy with a belt; his wife screamed at him to stop and Dennis ran from the house. It was the first and last time Joe attempted to exert his authority.

Aged twelve, Dennis was walking in Victoria Park, near his home, when he saw a boy drowning in the lake. He ran into the water and dragged the youngster to safety. It was a feat he was to perform on two more occasions. Once when he saved a friend, Paul Clay, from drowning in the Mediterranean, and once when he tried, and failed, to save a fellow escapee from a freezing Dartmoor reservoir.

On another occasion Dennis demonstrated courage of a different sort. He was leaving Barry's Dance Hall, in Hackney, when he saw a friend named Roy Harvey being attacked by a group of youths led by two teenage twins who would soon become notorious, Reggie and Ronnie Kray. He immediately ran to his friend's assistance and helped fight off the gang until the police arrived. After Ronnie and Reggie had been arrested and ended up in court, Dennis was called to give evidence against them. He insisted not being able to identify either of them, so the Krays walked free. Although Dennis insisted he had only attended court after being subpoenaed, Ronnie and Reggie bore a grudge against him and vowed to get their revenge. Something they may, indeed, have achieved in January 1967.

The Stafford's were, by this time, a prosperous family. Joe owned four racehorses - and Dennis was looked up to by other boys at Lauriston Road School. A friend, Walter Birch, told us: 'Dennis was always very friendly and used to invite me home for tea a lot. I looked on it as a great honour because his parents were so well-to-do.'

But, although financially secure, his parents were not wealthy enough for Dennis. He dreamed of making a fortune and living in luxury waited upon by servants. 'I was determined to make a million and buy Mum a mansion with a host of flunkeys,' he told his girlfriend, Pat Smithson in 1956.

After leaving school, at sixteen, Dennis became a waiter for a short time before partnering with a friend to set up a business renting out fruit-machines. Taking advantage of his inexperience, the man vanished one night with the firm's profits. Shortly afterwards Dennis was called up to do his National Service and served with the British Army of the Rhine, for two years. When he returned to civilian life, Dennis brought home a dangerous souvenir - a Luger pistol.

Joe, meanwhile, had sold his three-bedroomed home in Hackney and taken over the Duke of Wellington, a public house near Spitalfields Market. When he left the army, Dennis helped his father manage the pub, while spending more and more time in West End clubs, mainly in the company of criminals. Attracted by fast cars and glamorous women, desperate to make a lot of money fast, Dennis soon slipped into crime himself. He shared a flat in the West End with another man who, unknown to him, was a police informer.

Details of his first arrest vary depending on who is telling the story. According to Dennis, he became involved in a house-breaking and obtained some jewellery to fence. He asked his flat mate to arrange things and the man immediately telephoned the police. That afternoon Dennis was drinking at the Moulton Club, in London's West End, when a uniformed policeman came in and asked if he owned a car parked outside. Despite knowing the vehicle was stolen, Dennis agreed it was his. The policeman politely asked him to move the car as it was causing an obstruction. Unsuspecting, he left the club to do so. The moment he got behind the wheel; three plainclothes detectives climbed into the car.

They said they knew it was stolen and ordered him to drive them to West End Central police station. At this point, Dennis alleges, one of the officers opened the glove compartment and produced the Luger, saying, 'You're in real trouble now, boy.'

He had kept the weapon, his souvenir from National Service in Germany, in his flat and insists he never carried it in public and alleges it must have been planted by the police. There seems to have been substance to his allegation, since the matter was later raised in Parliament. At his trial he pleaded guilty in the expectation that this, together with his relative youth, he was only twenty-two, would lead to a light sentence. In the event he was given seven years imprisonment. As he collected his prison uniform from the trusty at Wormwood Scrubs, his initial, numb, disbelief gave way to bitter resentment and a determination to show people that he was far smarter than the society which had sentenced him.

'I felt the whole world was against me. Can you blame me for making up my mind to escape?'

The question was addressed to his girlfriend Pat Smithson, but it might just as well have been directed to the public at large. His answer would be to demonstrate his superiority in terms of intelligence, impudence and ice-cold nerve. He started well, with a cartoon-comic escape from prison. On November 8, 1956, Dennis and another prisoner, Anthony Hawkes who was serving a six-year sentence for fraud, made duplicate keys to the brush shop where Dennis worked. During the rest and recreation period, between 6 pm and 8 pm, they broke in and stole two prison officers' duffle coats, and a thirty-foot wooden ladder. Wearing the coats over their prison uniforms, they carried the ladder openly across the prison yard, propped it against the outside wall and coolly climbed to freedom. Jumping down from the wall they walked to the main road, hailed a cab and told the driver to take them to a flat in the West End, where Dennis had hidden £200 against such an emergency.

From there, he told us, they contacted an underworld organisation called The Link', which helps escaping prisoners. He was given a loan of £2,600 to start a new life and left with Hawkes for Newcastle, arriving on November 10. Posing as Paul Lewis, a Rhodesian businessman, with Hawkes, calling himself William Whelby, they rented rooms in a boarding house in St Thomas's Street. The landlady remembered them as quietly spoken young men who paid in advance for the rooms, wore expensive suits, drove a large black car and always behaved like perfect gentlemen.

The day they arrived, Paul Lewis and William Whelby called on a local estate agent and said they were interested in renting office accommodation. In Pink Lane, a narrow street leading up from the Central Railway Station, they found just what they wanted; a spacious, first-floor, office suite. Within forty-eight hours of scrambling over the wall at Wormwood Scrubs, the wanted men had transformed themselves into respectable Newcastle businessmen.

Next morning a sign-writer was commissioned to inscribe the firm's name on the office door. They called their non-existent company 'Onalbourne Ltd' and described themselves as: 'Merchants, manufacturers and mail order suppliers in gentlemen's wear, house textiles and novelties.' Furniture and stock were acquired, mostly on credit and the two men were ready to start trading. They had excellent bank references,' explained one of the suppliers a few months later when the truth about Paul and William came out. 'What more could you ask than that?'

Anthony Hawkes knew a great deal about the business, but as he had been jailed for forgery and fraudulent conversion of textile goods, he felt it wiser to stay in a back office when customers called. Dennis Stafford did the buying and made the contacts, travelling widely throughout the area he eventually acquired stock worth £5,000, about £86,000 in today's money. Some was stored in Newcastle, the rest in a London warehouse. Business prospered. With a slick line of commercial patter and expensively printed notepaper, Paul Lewis rapidly gained the reputation, especially amongst his competitors, of being a business genius. They couldn't understand how he was able to undercut them so drastically and still make a handsome profit.

The answer was that Lewis and Whelby were involved in what is called a long-firm fraud. This involves buying goods on credit and selling them below cost price. The trick lies in staying one jump ahead of your creditors for as long as possible.

As Onalbourne expanded more staff were engaged, amongst them fifty-three-year-old Gerald Hutton. After answering an advertisement in the local paper, he was taken on, as a salesman, at £3 a week, plus expenses and a three per cent commission. Sales were so good at the time he was delighted by these terms, later describing his bosses as: 'Charming. Ideal employers.'

Among Onalbourne's satisfied clients was the wife of a senior Newcastle-upon Tyne police officer. She was so pleased with the price and quality of some brocade Lewis sold her, she invited him to dinner with her husband. Lewis, always the perfect gentleman, smilingly accepted. Nor was this his only contact with the police force. As a leading businessman he was an honoured guest at the annual police ball.

Three weeks after arriving in Newcastle, Lewis and Whelby had left their St Thomas' Street boarding house and moved into two apartments in Osborne Road, paying six months' rent in advance. Paul Lewis entertained lavishly. He wined and dined top company executives in Newcastle's best restaurants and, more intimately, in the privacy of his luxury flat.

Both men were enthusiastic womanisers. A taxi-driver told us that in four weeks he took fifteen girls to Paul Lewis's flat. A police officer said there had been thirty women in Stafford's life at the same time. Among the girls, some of the most beautiful in the City, was Pat Smithson, a twenty-one-year-old office worker from Gateshead. One night, as she lay on the deep sofa in Lewis's flat, listening to the gramophone endlessly playing his favourite record Cindy, Oh Cindy, he revealed his true identity.

Dennis Stafford was supremely confident that he could go on outwitting the law well into the future. He might well have done, at least for a little while longer, but William Whelby brought things to a head. He withdrew the firm's total assets of £200 from the bank and vanished. When Hutton told Dennis, who was in Manchester on a buying trip, about his partner's disappearance he was instructed to sell all the remaining stock immediately. His boss explained that a big deal coming off and needed all the cash he could get his hands on. Before Hutton could carry out these instructions, a squad of police arrived at the Pink

Lane offices, apparently tipped off by an underworld informer. Dennis fled back south, leaving behind a wardrobe of expensive suits, some broken-hearted women, many furious creditors and several acutely embarrassed senior police officers.

Returning to London, Dennis lived in the West End while he made arrangements to leave the country. He didn't try to hide himself away. Indeed, he showed all the bravado and cool disregard for the police which had characterised his criminal career. One afternoon he strolled into Winston's Club, a favourite haunt of the Duke of Kent, ordered a lavish meal and a bottle of the best champagne for himself and a buxom blonde from the cabaret. Spotting a photographer, he called, the man over.

'Want a scoop?' he asked. As the camera clicked, he kissed the blonde full on the lips. A phone call from an informer alerted the police, who arrived in strength. Stafford eluded them via a rear window. Next day, his picture appeared on the front page of most national papers and the headline writers strongly criticised the police for allowing him to make fools of them for a second time. Hawkes was arrested in February, the following year, but Stafford had flown to Port of Spain, Trinidad. There he started a new life under the name of William Birch.

After being at liberty for nearly five months, he was finally arrested through a previous association with Eileen Cook, a blonde London hostess. On 22 March she cabled him: 'Meet me off BOAC Flight 463 Friday evening. Please meet me. I am not well. I love you. Even the GPO knows.'

Unknown to her, Eileen was being watched by police and the telegram was intercepted. A squad of policemen, led by Superintendent Conrad Fletcher, at once flew to Trinidad and Stafford was arrested in the airport terminal a few hours before Eileen's flight landed. After initially denying his true identity, Dennis finally admitted it, casually explaining to Conrad Fletcher, 'After flying 3,000 miles to escape arrest you don't expect me to identify myself to the first copper who asks, do you?'

In jail, he managed to make fresh headlines in the British press by going on a hunger strike, while unsuccessfully appealing against the extradition order. On 5 June two Flying Squad officers went out to Trinidad to bring him home. Their aircraft was delayed and rerouted, so it wasn't until 10 June that Stafford arrived home in England to be met by a large crowd of enthusiastic fans and scores of photographers and journalists. Stepping down from the plane, handcuffed and a smart grey suit, he raised a chained wrist high into the air for photographers and remarked: 'It's nice to be back, but I don't like the weather.' His impudent greeting made headlines around the world. Even the weather seemingly took note. The rain stopped and a heat wave began.

Escape from Dartmoor

Newcastle-upon-Tyne detectives escorted him back to Newcastle. There Dennis was sent to the Assizes on charges of conspiracy to defraud and obtaining goods by false pretences. Sentenced to a further eighteen months, he was sent to Dartmoor maximum security prison as a high security risk prisoner. It made no difference.

Six months later he again escaped, in the company of another prisoner, thirty-year-old William Joseph Day. They forced a window in the prison workshop and used a makeshift ladder to scale the 20ft outer wall. A warder spotted Stafford on top of the wall, but by the time he raised the alarm the two men had fled onto the mist.

More than a 1,000 police and special constables combed the snow-covered moor in the hope of recapturing them. At one point, cornered by police dogs, they plunged into an ice-covered reservoir. The police later found Day's body stretched on the bank. It was apparent that Dennis had made every effort to save him from drowning.

Despite numerous police roadblocks, Dennis got back to London and the bright lights of clubland. This time he was only free for six weeks before being recognized and arrested by a plain-clothes police sergeant. Sent to Wakefield Prison, he served the rest of his sentence without incident. In October 1962 he was allowed out, under strong escort, to marry his Gateshead girlfriend, Pat Smithson.

When he was released, in March 1964, Joe Stafford assured reporters his son was determined to become an honest, law-abiding, citizen. Dennis changed his name to Fielding and took a job as a £20-a-week salesman. His new life soon proved too dull and he was sacked after only a few weeks. On 7 September, that year, he received a twelve-month jail sentence for theft and the following November another six months for possessing a pistol within five years of release from prison. Free again at the start of 1966 he found work as manager of a Soho nightclub, before returning to Newcastle, at the invitation of Vince Landa, to take over as the new manager of The Piccadilly Club. With him came his latest girlfriend, the talented young black American singer, Selena Jones. Courtesy of his friends in the council, Landa gave the couple a new council house in Westmorland Rise, Peterlee. They shared their home with Selena's young housekeeper Lilian Bunker.

After the Fire

With the Piccadilly Club destroyed by fire, Dennis might have been out of work. But Vince offered him a new job booking cabaret acts for other clubs. He was to be paid £25 a week plus commission which he later said varied between £5 and £25 per week. Most all his household expenses were being paid by Selena Jones who was making a good living as a nightclub singer. She drove a white Mercedes while Stafford was given a company car, a Fiat 2300S coupe, formerly used by Angus Sibbet.

Over the weeks that followed, Michael, and Pat Burgess, who had also worked at the Piccadilly Club became regular visitors at Westmorland Rise and often spent the night there. It was there, at 10.30 on the night of January 7, two days after the murder, that he and Michael were arrested and charged with the murder of Angus Stuart Sibbet.

Chapter Six: A Night at the Birdcage Club

"If you think ...they have told you the truth about their going to Newcastle round about midnight, then you would not hesitate to find them Not Guilty.' Mr Justice O'Connor

On Tuesday 3 January 1967, Vince, Michael and their parents flew home from a Christmas holiday in Majorca. With them was Michael's girlfriend, Pat Burgess, and Dennis Stafford. Vince's wife Gwen, and their children, stayed behind. One of their sons, Dean, had been rushed to hospital with a burst appendix and his mother wanted to be with him while her husband was out of the country, dealing with urgent business in London. He had promised to return within a couple of days.

While waiting at Heathrow, for a flight to Newcastle, Michael telephoned the offices of Social Club Services to find out whether there would be any transport for them at the Newcastle Airport. Just before leaving for Majorca his car had been damaged in an accident and was being repaired in London. Dennis Stafford's second-hand Fiat 2300S coupe, a company car formerly used by Angus Sibbet, was being overhauled and resprayed at the Wheatsheaf Service Station in Sunderland. Michael learned neither vehicle was available, but Stanley Robinson, a director of the Wheatsheaf and of Social Club Services, offered to pick them up from Newcastle airport. Landa was staying in London overnight for a meeting with the company accountants, before flying back to Majorca the following afternoon.

The others flew directly to Newcastle. At the airport, Stanley Robinson was waiting, as promised, and drove them all to Chelsea Grove. From there, Michael's cousin Brian Ginger, took Dennis to his wife's home in Gateshead. He wanted to give his children the Christmas presents he had bought in Majorca. By this time, it was late evening and, having no transport, Dennis stayed overnight at Gateshead. Michael had arranged to collect him at 9.30 the following morning. In the event he was delayed, and he did not arrive until eleven. Tired of waiting, Dennis went a few doors down the street to a barber's shop. Before he could start his hair cut, Michael arrived and Dennis left the shop, telling the barber he would be back later. They then drove to Social Club Service's office in Low Row, Sunderland, where Michael met up with Angus to discuss business deals, he had left with him to sort out over the holiday.

Angus invited Michael to meet up with him at La Dolce Vita that night. Michael wasn't keen on the idea because the noise made it hard to have a serious business discussion. During his trial, Michael's counsel, Raymond Dean, asked him:

'What did you arrange between you and Mr Sibbet?'
'Well, it was not a definite arrangement.'
'What was suggested?'

'At the Dolce Vita we never discussed any business, the Dolce Vita being very packed and very noisy, and usually he had a lot of guests with him. So, it was not a very suitable place to discuss anything with him. I said to him we could meet in the Birdcage...he said, 'Will you be able to come?' and I said, 'I am not quite sure because I may have to go to Darlington,' and it was agreed I ring him up at five o'clock in the afternoon to say whether yes or no.'

Before leaving the office, Michael made a phone call to Vince, in London, to report on the morning's business. During their conversation he mentioned the problem of transport for Dennis, whose Fiat would not be ready for collection until Saturday. Since he was not going to be back in England until the following Monday, Vince agreed Dennis could borrow his red E-Type Jaguar. He then asked for information about Social Club Services' accounts. Michael said he would telephone this through to him at two o'clock, that afternoon, after visiting the account's office in John Street, Sunderland.

At about one thirty, the three of them left Low Row and were driven to their John Street offices in by Albert Ginley. Michael collected the information his brother wanted and called him, around two o'clock. According to Michael, Vince was about to board the aircraft for his return flight to Majorca and said he would telephone him at Chelsea Grove around midnight. After leaving John Street, at about two thirty, Ginley drove them to the Wheatsheaf Service Station where Vince's E-Type had been taken for servicing shortly before Christmas. The garage manager, Arthur Rowley, who had been instructed to release the car only to Vince Landa initially refused Michael's request to take the car. It was only after Dennis produced a key that Rowley shrugged and said: 'OK, take it.'

Dennis and the Spare Car Key

As things turned out it was singularly unfortunate Dennis should have this key. In its absence Rowley insists he would never have handed over the vehicle and the two men would never have been charged with murder. Asked in court to explain his possession of the key, Dennis explained that, about a week before going to Majorca, he had flown down to London to see his parents and visit his tailors. At Newcastle Airport he noticed the E-Type parked outside and mentioned this to Landa when they met up at Heathrow. Vince asked him to have it picked up, and Stafford telephoned a Mrs Richardson who worked at a local garage. She told him she would attempt to have it collected and taken to the Wheatsheaf to be serviced and stored. Because Mrs Robinson sounded uncertain whether or not this could be done, Stafford obtained the key number from Landa and purchased a duplicate. With this he could, if necessary, pick the car up when he returned to Newcastle in a couple of days. In the event, Mrs Richardson did as she was asked. The car was delivered to the Wheatsheaf and Dennis was left with a spare key.

They collected the E-Type and drove back to Low Row. About three o'clock, Selena Jones arrived. She had been in hospital over Christmas and unable to go with them to Majorca. After further business discussions, the three went around to a local wholesale store where Dennis wanted to complain about a recently purchased radiogram.

By five o'clock Michael and Dennis, who had missed lunch, were feeling hungry so they all went to the nearby 'Biz-Bar' for a meal. As soon as Michael had ordered a meal, he went outside to a public phone box to telephone Sibbet at his home in Dunston. He spoke first to Sibbet's wife, Brenda, and then to Angus himself. According to Michael they confirmed the meeting at the Birdcage for twelve thirty that night. While the only evidence the court heard concerning this arrangement came from the accused, this is not surprising. Had Angus mentioned it to anybody, that person's testimony would most likely have been hearsay and, therefore, inadmissible. He did, however, leave a note saying he was going to meet 'Mick' at Shiny Row, a village in Houghton-le-Spring. We will be returning to this note a little later.

The Events of that Night

After the meal, they returned to Low Row where they stayed until about six o'clock when Dennis and Selena left for their home in Peterlee. Michael went to a pub next to the office to discuss the day's business with another employee and stayed until about eight o'clock. He then drove the Arcadian to Denton, a Newcastle suburb, to pick up Pat Burgess from her parents' home. She had just finished washing her hair when Michael arrived, so he went on to visit his own parents, calling back for her at about ten o'clock. They then drove to Westmorland Rise, Peterlee. Pat was a friend of Selena's and wanted to find out how she was after her spell in hospital. She was also nervous about spending the night alone at Chelsea Grove. It was not certain that their housemate, Brian Ginger, would be at home and, recently, three of the houses in their street had been burgled.

Michael and Pat arrived at Dennis' home around 10.35. He parked the Arcadian, behind Selena's white Mercedes and Vince's red E-Type in the short cul-de-sac behind the house. Inside were Dennis, Selena and a Lilian Bunker, her housekeeper and companion, who had lived there for two months. Up to this moment, everything the accused said about their movements was corroborated, in virtually every respect, by both prosecution and defence witnesses. There was no conflict or dispute. But from this point on, if we are to accept the prosecution theory, all five Peterlee witnesses began to lie.

According to the police Stafford, when answering questions about his movements, said he left Westmorland Rise at eleven o'clock. This is flatly denied by Dennis himself and his solicitor, Graham Andrews, who was present during the interview. All claimed he clearly stated leaving home around 11.30. This is supported by Pat Burgess, Selena Jones, Lilian Bunker, and, of course, Michael Luvaglio.

The significance of this, so far as the police's theory about the accused's movements on the night of the 4th January is concerned, will be considered later. For the moment let's review the subsequent events of that night according to the defence evidence. At the trial Dennis Stafford gave the following account of his movements when being examined by his counsel, Rudolph Lyons:

'About what time was it that Michael came with Pat Burgess?'
'Well, as I said initially it was between ten thirty and eleven o'clock because I was watching this film that was on, Sir'.
'What was the name of the film?'
'What Lola Wants'.
'And what did you do after they came?'
'Well, Lilian made some tea and had a snack, a biscuit or something, and afterwards I went up and had a wash and, you know, prior to watching the wrestling etc.'
'Did you watch anything else on television?'
'Well, there was some political thing on, which I turned over to the ITV and there was some wrestling on. I always watch the wrestling'.
'Now, what time was it when you left?'
'I thought about eleven thirtyish, or after, you know, Sir.'
'Why do you think it was about eleven thirtyish?'
'I gauged that we had to get to Newcastle for twelve, and, therefore, as I told the police, I left myself about half an hour to get there.'
'You went out. Which car did you take?'
'The red and black E-Type, Sir.'
'Why did you go in that car?'
'There is only two of us going there and the Arcadian is like a big hearse and it was freezing cold and it was a very cold night, and the heater didn't work.'
Dennis went on to say that they drove to Newcastle via Sunderland and arrived at Chelsea Grove just after midnight, to await Vince Landa's call from Majorca. This account of their movements between eleven o'clock and midnight is substantiated by five witnesses, three at Peterlee and two at Chelsea Grove.
Pat Burgess told the court that she and Michael arrived at Westmorland Rise between 10.30 and 10.45. She knew Michael was going to meet Angus Sibbet later that night, but no other details of the meeting. She thought Dennis and Michael left the house again between 11.40 and 11.50. Selena Jones said, in evidence, that Pat and Michael arrived about 10.30 and talked of the holiday in Majorca until Michael and Dennis left the house between 11.30 and 11.45.
Lilian Bunker's testimony was equally unequivocal. Mr Taylor for the defence asked her:
'Can you say about what time they left?'

'About eleven forty-five.'

'Did you actually see them go?'

'Yes.'

Under cross-examination by Mr Scott she again said:

'They came in at ten forty-five and left between eleven thirty and eleven for-ty-five.'

'They came at ten thirty, didn't they?'

'A few minutes before a quarter to eleven'.

'How do you know that?'

'I heard somebody pull up outside.'

'How do you know what the time was? Did you look at the clock?'

'Yes, I naturally wondered who was coming at that time, so I looked at the clock.'

'And what did it say, ten forty-five?'

'A couple of minutes just before a quarter to eleven.'

'Were you watching television at that time?'

'Yes'.

'What was it?'

'I think we had just finished watching the film, or something, and then wrestling came on shortly after that.'

'And were you watching wrestling when they came in?'

'I cannot remember whether it was on then or not.'

'You saw the police and made a statement to them on the Friday, didn't you?'

'Yes, that's right.'

These were the answers of a young girl under close cross-examination in the tense atmosphere of a murder trial. By March, when called to give evidence, Lilian Bunker no longer worked for Selena and had only done so, in any event, for about ten weeks. Under the circumstances it seems unlikely that she should perjure herself so consistently and so well on behalf of the accused.

Pat Burgess and Selena Jones clearly would have had stronger motives to lie. But all three made statements to the police on 6 January, well before they knew anything of the prosecution evidence. Had they intended to set up a false alibi, they could not then have known whether or not the police might have had irrefutable evidence that they were lying. Again, if their evidence is all lies, they must have been told what to say by the accused who, had they killed Sibbet, would have known exactly what time he died and exactly what time to bracket with an alibi for themselves. As we shall see it would have been much better, and the murderers would have been aware of this, to establish that they left the house as late as twelve o'clock.

In addition to these three, who confirmed that Stafford and Luvaglio left the house at around 11.45, there are three further witnesses who saw the red E-Type, or an identical one, outside Chelsea Grove at about midnight. Of these only two were called to give evidence.

The first is Gladys Hill, a housewife living next door to Michael and Pat, at 7 Chelsea Grove. Gladys, who worked as a stewardess at the Excel Bowling Club in Westgate Road, told the court how, on 4 January, she had left work, with her daughter, Pat, about midnight. Mr Taylor asked her:

'About twelve o'clock, what, when you left the club?'
'Yes almost twelve o'clock, at midnight.'
'How many minutes' walk is it from the club to your house?'
'Well, I would say five to seven minutes.'
'Yes, and you went directly did you?'
'We came straight home.'
'So, what? Five, seven minutes past twelve, something like that you arrived home?'
'Yes, it would be.'
'As you approached your home did you notice anything about the vehicles in the street?'
'Well, there were cars in the street.'
'Yes, and outside the immediate vicinity of your house, and the one next door, what cars were there?'
'There were two cars.'
'Yes, is one of them - well ... is one of them there very, very, frequently?'
'One is there very frequently.'
'What sort of car is that?'
'I would say it is a large, beigey, bronze colour, er ... I don't know ...'
'Do you know what make or not?'
'No, I don't know.'
'Do you now whose car it is?'
'As far as I know it belongs to the gentleman who is using it now, er, Mr - er - the gentleman who is in the house next to me at the moment.'
Gladys Hill was then asked about a second car parked outside the house at that time.
'Can you describe that other car?'
'Well, it is a small - it was smaller than the first car.... It was broad but low and had a black top, a coupe type that you could turn over. Soft, that you could turn down.'
'And the colour?'
'The colour was cherry red, I would say...I don't know the make but to me it would be a sports car'. She added noticing that the light was on in the downstairs living room at Number 5.

The second witness, to have seen the E-Type at Chelsea Grove that night, was Robert Arthur Anderson, a company director, living at 19 Bishop's Avenue, Newcastle. He garaged his own car in Mill Lane, the continuation of Chelsea Grove, across its junction with Westgate Road. That night, after the television programme he had been watching ended, at about 11.50, he drove his car the short distance to the garage. Raymond Dean asked him:

'In order to get to your garage in Mill Lane, what route do you take?'
'I pass through Chelsea Grove; Mill Lane is the junction of Chelsea Grove.'
'That is what I wanted to get at. You pass along Chelsea Grove, do you?'
'Yes.'
'Do you remember the day when the news was released or announced of this murder having been committed?'
'Yes.'
'On the previous night, before the news was announced, did you put your car away?'
'Yes.'
'Did you go along Chelsea Grove?'
'I did, yes. At about twelve o'clock or thereabouts.'
'Did you notice any vehicle in Chelsea Grove that you recognised?'
'I noticed the E-Type Jaguar was outside in Chelsea Grove. I took it to be Mr Landa's. I noticed the lights; it was with the lights and when I passed it, I slowed down to see if anybody was in it.'
In cross-examination, Henry Scott suggested that it might have been much later, about 12.30, when he saw the car. Mr Anderson refuted this, insisting that he had passed the E-type no later than 12.10.
'I know that I was indoors about twelve fifteen after parking the car I had been watching the television and I could recall the times from that.'
        If these two witnesses are correct then, as we shall see, the prosecution theory about the red E-Type's movements that night must be wrong. And if wrong then, for reasons we will explain a little later, the case against Stafford and Luvaglio collapses. Even if they are only approximately correct in their estimation of the time, they saw the sports car - and this was what both Crown and Judge O'Connor suggested - the theory still collapses.
        This leaves only two explanations.
        Either they were deliberately lying under oath or they were confused about the day they saw the car. This is what Henry Scott suggested when cross-examining Gladys Hill:

'Are you quite sure that it was on the fourth of January that you saw it outside that house?'
'Oh yes, it was definitely the fourth of January because of my being late with the dance evening.'
        In fact, the prosecution's own evidence combined to rule out any other date. As we have seen, the E-type had been stored at the Wheatsheaf Service Station since before Christmas. It was used on the night of the fourth and thereafter remained in police custody until after the trial.

Were they lying?

Robert Anderson knew Michael Luvaglio and Vince Landa, in his capacity as the director of a firm of heating engineers who had carried out work at Dryderdale Hall. But would this have been sufficient incentive for him to commit perjury in a murder trial? If that was the case, then it seems more probable he would have concocted a stronger story. By claiming, for example, that he saw Dennis and Michael either in the vehicle or leaving the house. As for Gladys Hill, at no stage did the Crown suggest she had lied. She had no connection with Dennis Stafford and of Luvaglio, she said only: 'I know him well enough. I think he has been there approximately well over a year and going in and out we have had many conversations.'

Stafford and Luvaglio say they were waiting, in the front room of Chelsea Grove for the call from Vince Landa in Majorca.

'How long did you remain in the house?' Stafford's counsel asked him.
'The most we could have been there was about fifteen minutes, Sir, at the most.'
'And where did you go then?'
'We went directly to the Birdcage, Sir.'
'What time do you think you arrived inside the Birdcage?'
'As I said to the police, the time it takes to drive from Chelsea Grove to the Birdcage, which is a matter of minutes. You could walk it in ten, so about twelve thirty, Sir.'

The Birdcage Club, on Stowell Street, was flanked by warehouses and factories. It's ground-floor frontage was windowless with two solid wooden doors flanked by close boarded wooden slats. Opposite the club is a wide alley leading to a private car park. When they arrived that night Stafford and Luvaglio left the E-Type opposite the club entrance, its bonnet a few yards from this alley. Leaving the sidelights on, they crossed the road and entered the club. Beyond the entrance to the four-storey building was a small, oblong reception area with a flight of steep stairs, facing the door, leading up to a bar, gaming room and lavatories. To the left of the stairs was the reception desk, and beyond that swing doors leading into a large bar and cabaret room.

In examination by Rudolph Lyons, Dennis described a minor incident which occurred as they entered the cabaret room.

'As I went to grab hold of one it swung open and hit me. The artists were coming out with their guitars and I bumped into one of them.'

The man Stafford had bumped into was John Michael McGarry who had been performing with his partner, James Robert Allen. Their act, billed as the 'Allen and James Duo', normally began at midnight and went on for between thirty and thirty-five minutes. That night James Allen had a stomach upset, so they cut out a couple of numbers and their encore, finishing between 12.20 and 12.30. As they reached the swing doors McGarry pushed at them, but the way was blocked by somebody just coming in. Mr Taylor asked James Allen:

'Did you see who that person was?'
'Yes. It was Dennis Stafford.'

Allen went on to explain that he knew Dennis from the days when they had performed at the Piccadilly Club. This was confirmed by John McGarry and by two witnesses for the prosecution. The first of these was the club doorman, Matthew Dean, who estimated the time of Stafford and Luvaglio's arrival at between 12.20 and 12.30. The second, club manager John Bowden, explained that while he had not seen the two arrive, he noticed them in the club very shortly after the cabaret ended. None of the witnesses at the club noticed anything about the accused's clothing or behaviour that was in any way out of the ordinary. Club manager John Bowden was asked about this by Mr Lyons:

'You saw them come in. Did you notice anything abnormal about them?'
'No, Sir, no.'
'What about their cleanliness?'
'They were clean.'
Doorman Matthew Dean was also questioned on this point:
'Did Mr Luvaglio and Mr Stafford seem clean to you?'
'Yes.'
'Did you see any mud on them at all, or anything like that?'
Dean replied that he had not.

According to Dennis Stafford, he and Michael then waited for Angus Sibbet to arrive. After about an hour Michael telephoned Doreen Hall's flat and asked her what had happened to him. Doreen confirmed this when examined by Mr Castle-Miller.

'Did the telephone ring?'
'Yes. At about twenty past one.'
'Who spoke to you?'
'Michael Luvaglio. He asked me if Angus was back and I said, no.'
'Did Michael Luvaglio say from where he was ringing you?
'The Birdcage.'

Still waiting for Sibbet to turn up at 1.45, Stafford and Luvaglio asked Bowden if they could have something to eat. He told them the kitchen was closed but offered to provide sandwiches and coffee, which they accepted. According to Dennis Stafford, at around two o'clock, he found he was out of cigarettes and went to get some from the E-Type. Although there was a machine inside the club, he had packets of duty-free cigarettes - from the Majorca trip - in the car.

Stafford left the club to fetch them, telling Matthew Dean he would only be a moment. Under examination by Mr Castle-Miller, the doorman told the court what happened next.

'About two seconds later he came back and said, 'Someone has hit the back of my car.' I went outside and had a look.'
'What light is there outside the Birdcage at that hour?'
'It is quite light because there is a light straight opposite. When I looked the back of the car had been hit by, you know, it was all battered in, the back.'
        The car had, apparently, been pushed forward by the impact of a collision and now stood some fifteen feet further along the road from where Dennis and Michael had parked it. The rear lights were gleaming white where the covers had been smashed and, on the snow, Matthew Dean noticed a set of tyre tracks. Raymond Dean asked him:

'You could see quite clearly in the freshly fallen snow, as I understand it, the tracks of another vehicle which apparently had collided with the back of the E-Type and then reversed away, is that right?'
'Yes.'
Cross-examined by Mr Lyons, he elaborated on the details.

'Immediately outside the entrance to the Birdcage Night Club there is a one-way street?'
'Yes.'
'And if you are standing in the front door looking out, the traffic comes towards the right?'
'Yes.'
'And just opposite there is a sort of back street or back lane running into this street?'
'It is a car park for the offices that are further over. I think it is The Mecca. I'm not quite sure.'
'And when you went out to see the car you said Mr Stafford made no comments, but you made the comments as to the track where the car had gone into the car, that there was a track showing that a car had apparently gone into the back of the Jaguar, that is what you thought anyway, that it had gone into the back of the Jaguar?'
'Yes.'
'Was the Jaguar at that time facing up the street, Stowell Street? Facing in its proper direction?'
'Yes.'
        It is not clear from the trial transcript, or perhaps from the position of the tracks observed that night, whether this second vehicle had come down Stowell Street or out of the alley. But Dean was, none the less, quite certain that a collision had taken place at that spot. The second thing he noticed, on the blanket of freshly fallen snow were black rubber seals from a rear light

assembly. Mr Lyons asked him:

'Did you pick them up?'
'Yes, I took one of them up and looked at it.'
'What did you do with it?'
'I just put it back.'

From Dean's testimony comes one other piece of evidence pointing to the idea that a collision of some sort had occurred in the time between the two men leaving the car, around 12.20, and the time Stafford went to collect his duty-free cigarettes at about 2.00 a.m. Because the club has no windows and the doors are solid wood, Dean hadn't been in a position to see any such accident. Castle-Miller asked him:

'Did you hear the sound of a collision or not?'
'Outside in the alley-way there is a tube, an iron tube outside in the alley-way. During the day and there's cars coming out of the alleyway, they often hit this metal and it makes the noise of metal hitting metal. I heard that noise that night but did not take it as anything you see.'
'How long before you went out...'

Before the prosecuting counsel could finish his questions, the judge Mr. Justice O'Connor, intervened:

'Just wait a minute. About how far away from your door is this bar in which cars bang from time to time?'
'About twenty yards or twenty-five yards.'
'Something which sticks up from the road or sticks out from the road?'
'It had been a lamp post and they have just laid it to the side... sometimes, when cars come close to the wall, they hit the metal with their wheels.'

Dean said that he heard this sound about twenty minutes before he went outside with Stafford. He confirmed that having gone into the club none of the guests could have left without him seeing them. Apart from two emergency fire escapes, which couldn't be used surreptitiously, the front doors were the only way in or out.

Before leaving, for the moment, the question of the E-Type there is one further point we must mention. When Dennis Stafford left the car, he didn't lock it for the perfectly good reason that it was a soft-top and on a previous occasion when he had locked such a vehicle, somebody had simply cut a hole in the material to steal the contents. He preferred not to take this risk with Landa's car. He also expected that the meeting with Sibbet wouldn't take long.

At about 2.15 am they left the club and drove back to Chelsea Grove to see if Landa had phoned. On the first occasion Luvaglio had used his key and opened the door without difficulty, but now the door wouldn't open, so he rang the bell to awaken his cousin Brian Ginger. Dennis Stafford explained, to the court, that before they went on holiday burglars had used a crowbar to force open Michael's front door. The bottom lock had been broken off and the top one, a Yale, had been bent back splitting the wood. When it was replaced, the screws caught on the door.

After ringing the bell. Michael shoved at the door which suddenly opened. As they entered the house, Brian Ginger came downstairs and told him there hadn't been any calls. Michael replied he was going back to Peterlee to stay with Dennis. On arrival, they parked the E-Type in the garage, and went to bed. The following morning, Dennis inspected the damage and was relieved to see it wasn't especially serious. The rear number-plate was bent, paint had been chipped and the cover glasses were missing off both lights. Collecting some suits and shirts which needed cleaning, together with his laundry from the Majorca trip, Dennis put them in the boot of the E-Type and drove to the Zip Cleaners in the town centre. He was well known to the manageress, Mary Crammen, as both he and Selena were good customers.

Dennis and Michael then drove to Sunderland. Knowing that Landa was coming back from Majorca the following Monday and would expect to find the E-Type in perfect condition, Stafford went straight to the Wheatsheaf Service Station arriving about ten o'clock. He told Arthur Rowley that there had been an accident outside the Birdcage and that the car had been bumped and damaged. They asked if it could be quickly repaired and Rowley told them he would do the best he could. As the Wheatsheaf didn't employ panel beaters the car would have to be taken to Roker Car Sprays Limited, in Sunderland, to be repaired. Dennis left the vehicle and one of Rowley's men drove it to the repair shop. That evening it was removed by the police, before any work had been started.

According to Stafford's account it was later that morning, while he and Luvaglio were working in the offices of Social Club Services, they heard the news Sibbet's murder. Reporters had begun to phone Vince Landa for comment. They told him Sibbet's body had been found in a Mark X and that he had been battered to death. One of the journalists added there would probably be details in the television news that evening. Knowing that Rowley had a set in his flat, Michael and Dennis went to the garage and asked if they could watch it. When the bulletin confirmed Sibbet's violent death the effect on Michael Luvaglio was dramatic. He almost fainted and had to be given a glass of water and two tranquillisers by Rowley's wife. The two men returned to Peterlee where Luvaglio felt so shocked that he went to bed at seven o'clock.

Dennis was also in bed when, at 10.20, there was a knock on the front door. Putting on a dressing-gown, he went downstairs to open it. In the entrance stood Detective Superintendent John George Collinson of the Regional Crime Squad. He announced his identity and said: 'I must ask you to accompany me to Peterlee police station in order to assist in inquiries which are being made concerning the death of Angus Stuart Sibbet.'

Dennis and Michael got dressed and followed the officer to the police car. At the time neither was especially concerned. As Michael told us: 'We hadn't done anything, so we thought it was just a formality and that there was nothing to worry about.'

They could not have been more wrong.

Chapter Seven: Superintendent Kell Takes Charge

'Is that the piece of paper you used for writing up your notebook? One side is blank completely and the other contains four columns of writing ...and that is the result of an interview of one and a quarter hour without a break?'
'Yes, Sir.' Superintendent Ronald Kell answering under cross-examination.

The first policeman on the scene, as we explained in Chapter One, was Maurice Cluer the local South Hetton constable. Roused from sleep, he hurriedly pulled on his uniform and ran to the bridge from his home nearby. According to Cluer's account, the front of the Mark X was damaged with only its sidelights glowing weakly. Reaching in through the door he felt for a pulse in Sibbet's left wrist but detected no sign of life. With nothing more they could do, the small group of men waited in the snow, stamping their feet against the numbing cold of a January night where the temperature was six degrees below freezing.

More officers soon arrived, together with a police photographer who began taking pictures of the car and surrounding area. Using a large format plate camera on a tripod, he had to give each image a lengthy time exposure as no police lamps had yet been set up to flood the crime scene with light. Perhaps due to this limitation he took surprisingly few pictures of the Mark X, and none at all of Sibbet's body at the scene. These pictures had to wait for several hours, by which time the car had been towed to Peterlee police station. Sibbet's corpse was temporarily removed and then replaced, together with glass shards, once a protective plastic sheets had been spread over the seat.

The photographer was still at work when a local GP, Dr John Seymour Hunter, reached the scene from his home a mile away. He had been woken by a police officer at 5.40 am and arrived in a patrol car ten minutes later. The doctor waited a few minutes, for him to finish, before making a brief examination of the body.
Since he was the first medical expert to examine the dead man, and no other examination was made until seven hours later, when pathologist Dr Jack Ennis carried out a post-mortem in the Peterlee mortuary, Dr Hunter's observations are of great significance. Particularly because, as will become clear later, an accurate estimation of the time of death was to prove of vital importance to the prosecution case.

It is with his cursory examination we come up against the first piece of directly contradictory evidence. When Leslie Marshall saw the body, Dr Hunter examined it and the police photograph was taken, the dead man's left leg was bent. Yet miner Tom Leak clearly remembered that, when he opened the offside car door the left leg lay straight out along the seat with, as we mentioned above, his right leg drooping into the well. When we talked to him, only a few weeks after the trial, he repeated this description and even demonstrated the position of the leg while lying on his living-room sofa. At the trial he was equally certain about this, as an exchange with Michael Luvaglio's counsel, Raymond Dean, QC made clear.

'Would you look again at photograph No. 3, Mr Leak' he asked the witness. 'You see how the body is shown in that photograph with the knees bent and the left leg uppermost. How were the legs when you saw them?
'To me, which way I recollect. Sir, this left leg was full length on the seat'.
'Straight along the seat?'
'Straight along the seat'.
'Not bent?'
'Not bent like that. Not the way I remember it, Sir'.
'Did you bend it, or did you lift it?'
'No, I did not bend it'.
'You just lifted it?'
'I just lifted it.'

The importance of these conflicting observations will be fully examined in a later chapter. Briefly, the key point is that the condition of the dead man's left leg was the sole basis for Dr Hunter's assumption that rigor mortis was present at 5.50 am. In court he explained he had taken hold of the left leg 'and raised it slightly to ascertain the presence of rigor mortis.'

His opinion strongly influenced the police pathologist, Dr Ennis' estimation of the time of death. It caused him to change the time bracket, which he had given to magistrates at the committal proceedings, from a period when it would have been impossible for the accused to have murdered Sibbet to an earlier time bracket when they could just about have done so.

By six, Superintendent Ronald Kell had arrived to take charge of the murder inquiry. A 46-year-old, Kell joined the police at the age of 26, after serving in the Royal Navy during the Second Wold War. He was a detective who rapidly made up his mind about a case and was then reluctant to change it. This, as we will see later, sometimes led him to make costly blunders.

A man of strong opinions Kell, like many ex-servicemen in the 'sixties, had risen rapidly through the ranks. While believing he had a strong 'copper's nose' for detecting a villain, he also prided himself on adopting a scientific approach to detection. He had been one of the first police officers in the North-East to attend a newly created forensic science course.

At 7.30, red paint fragments from the damaged Mark X bumper were collected by Superintendent Arthur Chapman. Dr Jack Ennis, police pathologist, started his preliminary investigation shortly after eight, but conducted only a brief examination, leaving the main work until the body had been delivered to his mortuary.

Detective Sergeant Frank Morgan, of the Serious Incident Squad, was told to organise a towing vehicle to take the car to Peterlee police station. This proved more difficult than expected and it was not until after eleven that one finally arrived. This was not a low loader as might be expected, or even one which provided a rigid tow. Rather it allowed the Mark X to swing widely. It took the driver and his police escort two hours to complete a journey of less than five miles. Despite this snail-pace speed, the Mark X's radiator received further damage. This went unnoticed at the time but gave rise to awkward exchanges between Counsel and the Judge during the trial. What this damage was and why it mattered will be described later.

In the police yard, further pictures were taken before the body was wrapped in three large polythene sheets and transferred from the car to a plain van for the last stage of its journey to Easington mortuary where it arrived at noon. Sibbet was laid out on a stainless-steel table and undressed. At 1.15, in the presence of Detective Sergeant Morgan, Dr Ennis started his examination.

Sibbet's Post-Mortem

Three shots had been fired into the body at close range, with the fatal bullet entering just below the left shoulder. Penetrating vertically, it severed the aorta and ploughed through other vital organs before lodging in soft tissue above the right hip.

A second bullet entered just below the right nipple, passing downwards and outwards, coming to rest in the upper part of the right buttock. The third bullet went through the right wrist and right loin before exiting the body. It was found loose amongst the clothing.

In addition to the bullet wounds, there were superficial external injuries. Brush abrasions, approximately 50 cm wide, on each knee and another about three quarters of an inch long on the left ankle. There were scratches on the left side of the upper abdomen and further abrasions to the right side of the forehead.

The dead man's rectal temperature was 64 °F, down from a normal 98.4, and his limbs were fixed by rigor mortis. This led him to estimate the time of death as between 12 midnight and 4:00am on 5th January. Such an estimate is in line with accepted procedure, in which rate of temperature loss expected after death lies between 2.60 and 3.20 F per hour.

On this basis, taking the maximum temperature loss and minimum temperature of death, and vice versa, the extreme limits between which the victim had been dead at the time of the postmortem took place would be between 10.75 and 13.61 hours. Which meant he died between 11:39pm and 2:30am. Both in his report, and at the magistrate's court Dr Ennis stuck to this estimate. When it came to the trial, he conveniently altered the time of death so as to fit in with the persecution case.

Dr Ennis took samples of hair from all parts of the body, extracted the fingernails and collected blood, urine and four days after the autopsy these samples together with sixty-two items of Stafford's clothing, eleven of Luvaglio's and thirteen from Sibbet were delivered to Mr Norman Lee for scientific examination. He also received soil, grass and blood samples together with vacuum sweepings from inside both cars. We quote his report below in detail.

Norman Lee's Forensic Report

'The clothing shows bullet holes as follows: An absolutely simple hole through the overcoat, the jacket, the shirt and the braces, behind the left shoulder about midway between the neck and shoulder seam (Injury B1). A simple hole showing a downward direction through the right front of the overcoat, the jacket, the shirt, and the vest, fairly close to the mid-line of the chest and about mid-way between shoulder and waist levels (Injury B2). A simple hole through both the outer and inner aspects of the right cuffs of the overcoat and jacket; this hole shows as a nick in the edge of the right cuff of the shirt on the inner aspect (Injuries B3 and B4).

A very complex hole which is represented in the overcoat and jacket in the right front chest region near the right side and distinctly lower than (B) above and in the shirt and vest at about waist level in the back near the right side.

That part of the hole which is in the overcoat and jacket shows a steeply descending path. For this to be a single bullet hole the clothing must have been severely deranged [disturbed ? Our comment] i.e. either the shirt and vest right side pulled towards mid front or the right side of the jacket and overcoat pulled towards the mid back (Injuries B1 and B6)…Bloodstaining on the deceased's clothing is essentially associated with the bullet holes. I would expect most of it to have come after death and doubt if anybody handling or moving the body soon after the shooting would acquire much if any bloodstaining.

The Deceased's clothing also bears soil/mud staining and recent damage as follows: The overcoat has fairly superficial wet mud staining, especially on the sleeves and the left side of the shirt and on the inside of the lower left front. The trousers have fairly heavy wet mud scuffed into the cloth from the front mid waist across to the right thigh region with an isolated lighter area on the left thigh. There is no such soil staining on the knee regions. The front waist band shows dirt and scuff marking on the lining edge and parts of the two waist fasteners are missing. I recovered one of these adhering to blood on the vest, the other is still missing.

The shirt has fairly heavy wet mud scuffed into the cloth of the front over most of its length with lighter mud staining on the right sleeve and traces of the same on the left sleeve. The shoes show slight scuff marks and light mud staining on the tips of the toes. The heel of the left shoe bears recent deep impact damage which I am unable to explain.

The tie bears fairly heavy wet mud staining on both surfaces of each of the end pieces which hang below the knot. The vest bears fairly heavy wet mud staining on the front. This is essentially in a band from approximately just below the right breast to the left waist regions. On the left of this mud staining two recent small holes were probably caused by stones. This dirt and damage pattern on the clothing is indicative of the body having been dragged, both headfirst and feet first, quite possibly with a shunting type of motion.

His report ends: 'Grass debris recovered from several items, namely the overcoat, the trousers, the head hair and the radiator grilles is of little value; whilst there is a similarity between the species represented and the control sample I am quite certain that they could equally well have come from many other grassy patches.'

In summary, Lee's report concluded that Sibbet had been shot at close range and died almost instantly. His corpse had then been dragged across muddy grass before being manhandled into the rear of the Jaguar.

Sibbet was six feet tall and Dr Ennis estimated, although never measured, his weight at around 14 stone. Neither Dennis Stafford nor Michael Luvaglio are particularly strong and manoeuvring Angus' body into the back of a Mark X would have required considerable strength. All this would have had to be done in almost total darkness. The freezing cold January night was pitch black and there are no streetlights on that stretch of the A182, or in nearby Pesspool Lane, where the murder and the cleaning of the Jaguar are alleged to have taken place. Furthermore, for the police case to stand, the killing, dumping the body and cleaning the car must all have taken place in no more than four minutes.

Under these circumstances, one might reasonably expect some traces of blood, mud, grass, fragments of metal, slivers of plastic or broken window glass to be found on the accused's clothing or inside either the E-Type or the Mark X. Yet, despite the most detailed and painstaking examination not one of these items yielded any evidence of use to the police.

The Locard Exchange Principle

This flies in the face of a key tenet of forensic science, the Locard Exchange Principle. Named after Dr Edmond Locard, who set up France's first ever police laboratory in Lyon, just before the First World War. The Principle asserts whenever two objects, whether living or inanimate, come into contact there will always be a transfer of material between them. This may be blood, hairs, fibres, fluids, paint and skin particles transferred either from criminal to victim or victim to criminal. They may be found on skin or clothing, under fingernails or lodged in hair. Yet no traces of blood, mud, grass, fragments of metal, slivers of plastic or broken window glass was present on any of the accused's clothes.

If Stafford and Luvaglio did, indeed, carry out the killing they must rank as the first, and probably the only, murderers in history to have committed such a crime without any forensic traces being found.

The absence of exchange evidence is, in the view of many of the experts studying the case over the years extraordinary and highly significant. In court considerable consideration was given to this and serious doubts raised by defence counsel without this glaring discrepancy making any difference to the final verdict.

The Gun That Killed Angus Sibbet

On examining the dead man's overcoat, ballistics' expert George Price, found discharge residues around all three bullet entry holes. Remarkably he was never asked to test the clothing of the accused for such traces. In all the shooting cases we have investigated, there have been clear indications of a cloud of residues generated by the shot. The amount that can be detected on the killer's skin or clothing will depend on the circumstances in which the shot was fired, for example indoors or outdoors on a windy day.

While the lack of testing the hands of the accused may seem strange, we have to consider the validity of the tests available to forensic examiners in the 'sixties. The most widely used was the paraffin or dermal nitrate test. Introduced in the early 1930s soon widely used. The idea was to detect the presence of nitrate residues deposited on the hand of the assailant. This is deposited, when a gun is fired, by the smokeless powder used as a propellant in modern cartridges.

A paraffin wax cast is made of the suspect's hand and a reagent applied. The presence of nitrates is revealed if dark blue spots appear. Unfortunately, the test was notorious for creating 'false positive' results. Incorrectly asserting someone had fired a handgun when they had not. This was due to the tests non-specificity. One study reported a positive reaction is produced by tobacco or tobacco ash, fertilizer, rust, fingernail polishes, soap tap water and evaporated urine. While the test certainly detects nitrate residues the source of these cannot be determined.

'Consequently,' notes Paul Giannelli from the Case Western University School of Law, 'the probative value of a positive reaction is marginal at best. and, therefore, the paraffin test is rarely used today.

During the trial Mr Henry Scott, for the prosecution asked Mr Price what inference he drew from these gunshots, starting with the hole in the left shoulder.

He replied: 'This indicates to me that it arose through the discharge of a pistol from extremely close range, possibly about half an inch,' Price told him 'I have carried out test firings with ammunition of the same type as these bullets and cases and used a pistol of the type which I think could well have been used to fire these bullets and cases.'

'What is the next hole that you found?' Scott inquired.

'There is another similar hole on the right front just above this top button. This also shows an area of intense blackening and powdering.

It is a more confined area than the one behind the left shoulder, and I concluded this could well have been caused when the muzzle of the pistol was actually touching the overcoat.'

'Did you find another hole?'

'Another bullet entrance hole was present on the outer aspect of the right cuff. There is a corresponding exit hole on the inner aspect of the same cuff, in other words, the same bullet has possibly gone completely through the sleeve.'

'Could you estimate the range of that shot?'

'Yes, Sir, the entrance hole showed slight discharge residues and from this I concluded that the range was approximately three feet.'

'Did you find another?'

'Another bullet hole was present on the right front, further round to the right than the first one referred to. This shows no discharge residues at all...This bullet hole could well have arisen by virtue of the bullet that passed completely through the cuff having continued on its course and passed through the over-coat in this position...if the arm was across the front of the body.'

He identified the bullets in Sibbet's body, and bullet fragments found in the Mark X, as of 7.65 mm calibre probably fired from a self-loading pistol. Developed, in the late 19th century, by John Browning this type of bullet is known as the Browning Short as it was designed for use in their FN M1900 semi-automatic pistol. These cartridges can, however, be fired from several types of handgun, including Mauser and Walther.

No such weapon was found and there was no evidence that either Dennis or Michael ever possessed one.

George Price also examined the two bullet holes in the Mark X. The first was in the rear pillar of the off-side front door, the second in the veneer behind the driver's seat. All the shots had come from the same weapon. Discharge residues were found on the door pillar indicated that this shot had also been fired from very close range. No residues were associated with the second shot which had shattered the rear drivers-side window.

In the police yard at Peterlee, forensic scientist Norman Lee found a large area of blood, type AMM, on the front transmission tunnel carpet. This had come from neither of the accused nor the victim. Its source was never traced, and its presence ignored by both police and prosecution. They reported it but made no attempt to locate the source.

As we will explain in a moment, this was not the only unidentified blood associated with the case. This too was ignored when the police built their case against the accused

Anonymous Call Tips Off the Police

At 3.30 in the afternoon, on the day of the murder, police received a telephoned tip-off directing them to Dennis and Michael. The police would only say this was 'information received', which may well mean that they knew the identity of the informant. Detectives hurried to Roker Car Sprays in Sunderland where they seized Landa's E-Type Jaguar. The managing director assured them nothing had been done to the car since it was brought in earlier that day. A police guard was left by the vehicle and at 8.15 Detective Sergeant Morgan arrived to photograph damage to its rear end.

At 10.20 p.m. Detective Superintendent John Collinson arrived at Westmorland Rise, Peterlee. The door was opened to him by Dennis Stafford wearing pyjamas and a dressing gown. Michael Luvaglio was upstairs in bed. Collinson asked both men to accompany him to Peterlee police station which they did without protest.

Michael is Interviewed

Superintendent Kell questioned Michael Luvaglio first, with Detective Superintendent Mitchell taking notes. This interview lasted for fifty-five minutes. In describing what was said, Detective Superintendent Mitchell told Henry Scott:

'Asked by Superintendent Kell to give account of his movements on Wednesday 4 January, said he had returned to this country from Spain on Tuesday 3/1/67. Following day had gone to his office at Sunderland where he had seen Dennis Stafford among other people...Got to Peterlee about ten thirty p.m. and talked to Stafford and Selena until about eleven p.m. when he and Stafford left in the red E-Type. They had travelled to Newcastle and had called at his home in Chelsea Grove because he was expecting brother Vincent phoning from Majorca. Got to C. Grove between twelve p.m. and twelve fifteen a.m. and when no call was received went to the Birdcage Club arriving between twelve thirty and twelve forty am.'

Luvaglio went on to say they had stayed at the Birdcage, until about 2.15 am, then returned to Chelsea Grove to check if the phone call had come and that they had then driven home to Westmorland Rise arriving at about 3 am. He mentioned E-Type had been damaged while parked outside the Birdcage Club.

Dennis is Interviewed

At 1.49 am, in the presence of his solicitor Graham Andrews, Dennis Stafford was questioned by Kell. Once again Detective Superintendent Mitchell kept a note of what was said, but Andrews failed to do so. He explained to us he expected to be able to trust the accuracy of the police note.

As with Luvaglio's questioning there is no contradiction in anybody's version of what took place until they reached the moment of departure from Peterlee. At the trial Detective Sergeant Mitchell quoted Dennis's reply as follows:

'. . . stayed in the house until Luvaglio and Pat arrived then Luvaglio and he left house about 11 p.m. Travelled in E-Jag to Newcastle visiting Luvaglio's house in Chelsea Grove....'

The main purpose of these questions, Detective Superintendent Mitchell agreed, was to establish the movements of the accused on the night of 4/5 January. Luvaglio's counsel, Raymond Dean, asked him:

'You made a note on this piece of paper, exhibit 84. It is both sides of a single sheet of foolscap, is that right?
'Yes, Sir.'
'And how long did the interview take with Mr Luvaglio?'
'From twelve twenty to one fifteen. Sir.'
'I see, just fifty-five minutes.'
'Yes.'
'And this is the only note made, is it, during that interview?'
'Yes, Sir.'
'And there is no other?'
'No, Sir.'

As Raymond Dean established during his cross-examination, his notes on Superintendent Kell's interview with Dennis Stafford weren't any more detailed.

'Superintendent Kell, I wonder if you would now look at the paper on which Superintendent Mitchell made his notes. I am only asking you to look at the paper on which Superintendent Mitchell made his notes with regard to Mr Stafford, please, you now have them in your hand, is that right?'
'Yes, Sir.'
'Is that the paper you used for writing up your notebook?'
'Yes, Sir.'
'Now, would you just hold it up so that the jury may see it? One side is blank completely.'
'Yes, Sir.'
'The other side contains four columns of writing…and that is the result of an interview of one and a quarter hour without a break?
'Yes, Sir.'

Kell Charges Dennis and Michael

At three o'clock on the morning of January 6, less than twenty-two hours after the body had been found, Kell cautioned Dennis Stafford and Michael Luvaglio. He told them they were being detained on suspicion of the murder of Angus Sibbet. Luvaglio said nothing. Stafford retorted: 'It's ridiculous.'

At 9.40 pm, the same day, Kell decided that he had enough evidence to charge them both with murder and they appeared before Peterlee magistrates the following morning. Fifteen officers surrounded the small magistrates' court and a dog and handler patrolled the corridors for the few minutes which the hearing lasted.

So effectively had Sibbet positioned himself as a top man in the gambling world that the local paper's headline proclaimed: 'MEN ACCUSED OF GAMING BOSS MURDER'. Other stories warned of gangland involvement and hinted at attempts to free the accused. Appeared in the dock handcuffed to policemen, Stafford and Luvaglio were remanded in custody in Durham Prison.

While Superintendent Kell believed he had sufficient evidence to prefer the charges, the truth was he had next to none. No physical evidence has been collected, the murder scene remained to be identified, a post-mortem was yet to be conducted and no witnesses had been questioned.

As we explained earlier, Kell was a man who made up his mind a case rapidly and, having done so, stubbornly persisted in following that line of enquiry even in the face of contradictory evidence. This is well illustrated by a bungled murder investigation he had conducted the previous year.

A Housewife's Savage Killing

In December 1964, a 32-year-old housewife Patricia Parker was found dying of head injuries in the backyard of her home at Leadgate, near Consett. She had been savagely beaten with an iron bar and was discovered, by her 34-year-old husband John, left lying in a pool of blood. Kell became convinced, early on in his enquiry, that she had disturbed a man stealing coal stored in her yard and that he had panicked and killed her. With this in mind Kell instructed the thirty detectives under his command to interview 4,500 local people over a period of several weeks.

It took until March for the Superintendent to admit his mistake. As in 75% of such slayings this was a domestic murder. The husband, John Parker, was arrested, found guilty and jailed for life.

The waste of time and money the delay had created led to Kell being strongly criticised by his superiors. He may have hoped that, by solving the Sibbet murder in just a few hours he could redeem his reputation.

Another reason may have been the local and political pressure the police were under the bring the case to a swift conclusion. Headlines stressing possible the possible gangland connections of the accused had greatly increased public concern. T. Dan Smith and other leading council officials, concerned their corrupt practices might be exposed through links with Social Club Services, were eager to close down a potentially embarrassing in-vestigation. Given Smith's close connections to senior Labour Party politicians, they may have even been pressure from the top to bring someone to justice without delay.

Evidence is Gathered

During the weeks following the finding of Sibbet's body the A182, between South Hetton and its junction with Pesspool Lane was the scene of intense police activity. A few hours after Leak's discovery a roadblock was set up sealing off a long stretch of the main road, from just outside the village to beyond the Pesspool Lane junction.

As police, cadets and soldiers, some of them equipped with mine-detectors, searched the fields and ditches, all cars passing along this section of the main road were stopped. Drivers were asked the purpose of their journey and told not to park anywhere between the two checkpoints, while pedestrians were banned from using the road or footpaths. Detectives also examined timecards at South Hetton colliery to find out which workers would have been going on or off duty during what the police regarded as the critical period, between 11.00 pm and 5.15 the following morning. Posters with the bold, black heading MURDER appeared in shop windows and anybody who might have seen or heard anything unusual was asked to come forward. Twenty-one witnesses were found who had information about the movements of the Jaguars on the murder night and, of these, nine were chosen to give evidence. Among them was Tom Leak, the miner who had found Sibbet's body.

The same afternoon as the murder, he had taken his wife shopping in Sunderland. Returning home, they found detectives waiting to interview him. He spent several hours with them and made a statement. By the time committal proceedings started, it had become clear to the police that calling him would draw attention to the first of many inconsistencies in their case. To avoid this, they decided to call his friend Leslie Marshall whose testimony, they regarded as being more favourable to the prosecution. It was not until Tom had been asked to give evidence for the defence, that the prosecution changed their minds about him and Leak reluctantly agreed to appear as a witness for the Crown.

Among the first to respond to the police appeal, was farmer's wife Nora Burnip. She and her husband, lived at West Moor Farm, a two-storey, slate-roofed building some 260 yards from the A 182. Between nine-thirty and ten o'clock on the night of January 4, the couple had climbed the narrow staircase to their bedroom on the first floor. It was their custom to retire early and then read for a couple of hours in bed. At about midnight Mr Burnip reached over and switched off the bedside light, glancing at the alarm clock as he did so. He fell asleep, but his wife stayed awake and was suddenly startled by two sharp cracks. They were so loud and unexpected that she woke her husband, then got out of bed and crossed to the single, narrow window with its view over the farmyard, fields, and the A182, some 260 yards away. Uncertain from which direction the sounds had come, Nora drew the curtains and stared curiously into the black winter's night. About a third of her view along the road was obscured by a haystack between the house and highway.

She could not see anything unusual. No headlights moved on the A 182, nor was there any sign of activity. The strange sounds were not repeated. Puzzled, she went back to bed and fell asleep. It wasn't until the following day, when she learned of the murder, that Nora realised a possible explanation for what she had heard and contacted the police.

Nora Burnip's Evidence

On the afternoon of the first day, Nora Burnip entered the witness box, took the oath and faced her first question from Mr Henry Scott for the Crown. She told him about going to bed between nine-thirty and ten o'clock and reading.

'Do you remember, roughly, what time it was you stopped reading?'
'We had put the light out, I think, shortly before midnight'.
'And after you had put the light out did you hear anything?'
'Well, I said it was like two sharp cracks.'
'Yes. From somewhere outside the house?'
'Yes, a little distance away.'
'Which direction did they seem to be coming from?'
'Well, I really couldn't tell you.'

After some further questions about what she could have seen from the window Mr Scott asked her:

'And how long after you turned the lights out was it that you heard those two sharp cracks, roughly?'
'Roughly, well, getting on towards twenty past twelve, I should think.'
'You mean about half an hour - well, you turned the lights out, you said, a few minutes before twelve?'
'Yes.'
'So, it would be about twenty minutes after you turned the lights out that you heard them?'
'I should think so, yes.' 'Had you gone to sleep at all, or had you been awake all the time?
'I was awake all the time.'
'When you turned your lights out did you see the time on the clock or anything?'
'My husband looked at the time. I did not.'
'How long before the lights went out had he looked at the time?'
'He looked at the time when he put the light out.'
This was clearly a crucial piece of testimony for the defence, as Mr Lyons told her: 'You realise that it is important to my client, and the best you can do is you think it is about twenty past twelve?'
'I think so, yes ...'
'I know you cannot say definitely, but when you gave evidence last time, you did say, 'I think about twenty past twelve.'
'About twenty past.'
'Is that your honest view, although you cannot say for certain, about twenty past?'
'I think about twenty past.'

'Mrs Burnip, enough time had intervened between putting the light out and hearing the two sharp cracks for your husband to go off to sleep?'
'Oh, yes.'

Here was a witness called by the prosecution who could do nothing but discredit their theory. At no time, either during the committal proceedings, or in examination and cross-examination at the trial, did she waver. She only heard two shots, yet it was vital to the police theory that five were fired at the same spot, within seconds of one another, and at 11.50 not 12.20. But suppose those two cracks were unconnected with the murder – although it is hard to see what else could have caused them – and five shots were indeed fired at 11.50 p.m. Then surely Mr and Mrs Burnip, sitting up in bed reading, must have heard them, and probably the car crash as well. Their farm stands isolated in the middle of flat, deserted countryside, and the fairly strong wind blowing across the road would have carried the sounds in their direction.

She couldn't tell which direction the sounds had come from and saw nothing unusual on the A182. At that point, however, a haystack obscured her view of a large part of the road. As a result of her evidence, the police concentrated their search on this area and in near-by Pesspool Lane.

DC Tipler's Lucky Finds

At about 3.30 on the afternoon of January 7, Detective Constable Tipler discovered some red and amber Perspex fragments in the lane, together with a reflector, a small metal strip and a quantity of cigarette ends lying on the verge. The source of these was never identified and neither the prosecution nor the defence made any reference to them. Tobacco of another kind might also have featured in evidence, but the police made no reference to it, and indeed seemingly concealed all trace of it.

When the Mark X was photographed in the yard of Peterlee police station, a packet of Bahama Cigars can be seen below the glove compartment on the passenger side. Handmade, only in the Bahamas, these are a relatively rare and unusual brand and not one ever smoked by Stafford or either of the Luvaglios.

What happened to the cigars between the two photographs? A retired, Northumberland PC we interviewed remarked cynically. 'They probably smoked them. If they were anything like the Cleveland police, I'm surprised the Mark X even made it to the police station!'

The more charitable, and far more likely, explanation is that it was sent away for forensic analysis. If so any findings, or indeed any mention of the cigars at all was never presented in court by the prosecution nor disclosed to the defence.

Two days later the same officer was with another search party, this time on the A182. Towards the end of the afternoon he found pieces of clear glass, amber and red Perspex and a mirror-type reflector about a quarter of a mile east of South Hetton. The following day, Tipler collected a pair of spectacles and on 10 January further fragments of glass, flakes of red and green paint and a small part of the Mark X's front number-plate.

The same day, seven cartridge cases were found. Two on the left side of the road, as one faces towards Easington, another beside the kerb at the edge of a tarmac footpath, and the fourth a short distance away at the side of a verge beside the path. The remaining three were on the other side of the road, two balanced on the nine-inch-wide kerbstone and the third in the gutter eighteen feet away from the others.

Blood on the Phone Book

At 5.45 pm, on 6 January, Detective Constable Richardson called at the Zip Cleaners, Peterlee, and collected two suits and six shirts which Dennis Stafford had brought in for cleaning the previous morning. These, together with dozens of other items of clothing from Dennis and Michael Luvaglio, were sent to the Northern Forensic Laboratories for examination by Mr Lee. He also received one other rather curious item, the bloodstained page of a telephone directory from one of the two phone boxes in South Hetton. The same box from which miner Tom Leak had made his emergency call. The page was thickly covered with blood belonging to the same group as Angus Sibbet. A type found in only 20% of the population.

On the afternoon of the sixteenth, at an inquest on Sibbet, Dr Jack Ennis told the coroner that he estimated the time of death as being between twelve midnight and 4 am on 5 January.

Dennis Protests His Harsh Treatment

The accused appeared at Peterlee magistrates court on 24 January and, once again, Dennis Stafford's solicitor - Graham Andrews – again protested about his client's treatment in prison. According to Mr Andrews he was ... 'not even allowed to rest on his bunk during the day. If he sits on a chair or puts his feet on the bunk, he is told to put his feet down.'

Despite this, the two were further remanded until 30 January when Graham Andrews repeated his complaint that that Stafford was being treated harshly. 'He isn't even allowed a knife and fork to eat his meals,' he told the bench. If there was any other country in the world where a man was being held without trial under these conditions, Parliament would be up in arms against it.' The chairman of the magistrates, Mr Harry O'Neill, said there was nothing they could do except once again remand the accused in custody.

On Wednesday 8 February there was another remand and Mr Andrews told the court that Stafford was being kept in solitary confinement and not even allowed a radio in his cell.'

Some MPs took these allegations seriously and a question was asked in the House. Despite this the punitive conditions continued. The prison service, it seemed, had never forgiven the 'playboy fugitive' for the embarrassment he had caused them in the past and were determined to exact their revenge.

It was not until 16 February, following six weeks of investigations, that the police were ready to proceed. On the day of the magistrate's court hearing, people queued from early morning and, within minutes of the doors opening, the public gallery was crowded to capacity.

On Friday 18 February the defence made their submissions. For Dennis Stafford, Mr Steer said there was not one item of direct evidence of complicity nor was there any prima facie evidence that he was at the scene of the crime at the material time. Mr Taylor, for Michael Luvaglio, claimed there was no evidence to connect either Stafford or his client with the death of Sibbet.

The magistrates took a different view and sent both men for trial. But, possibly indicating the tenuous nature of the prosecution case, it was the decision took them two hours and twenty minutes to reach.

Chapter Eight: The Case for the Crown

'Clear proof of their guilt of the murder was established by a feat of brilliant and patient criminal investigation for which all concerned are to be very highly commended.'
Lord Justice Edmund Davies dismissing leave to appeal on 30 July 1968.

According to the police case, after leaving Peterlee, at about eleven o'clock on the night of January 4, Dennis Stafford and Michael Luvaglio drove along the A182, then turned onto the B1284 just north of South Hetton heading towards Newcastle. At some point along this road they met up with Sibbet, driving his Mark X, who had driven straight from La Dolce Vita. Both vehicles came to a halt and either Dennis or Michael got out and climbed in beside Sibbet. The E-Type was then turned around and led the Mark X, back on the A182 towards South Hetton. About half a mile past the village, near West Moor farm, the E-Type came to an abrupt halt and the saloon collided with the its rear.

As Sibbet got out of his car, either Dennis or Michael shot him shot three times, at close range. The two killers then manhandled his corpse onto the saloon's backseat, and one of them got behind wheel. The two cars then continued in convoy down the A182, before turning right into Pesspool Lane. A few hundred yards along this lonely, thorn-hedged road, they stopped, to clean out the saloon. They then drove on down the lane, through the village of Haswell, and re-joined the A 182 at north side of South Hetton. They retraced their earlier route through the village. Close to Pesspool Bridge the Mark X stalled due to overheating from damaged to the radiator received in the collision. Panicking, the killers abandoned the saloon, leaving the sidelights, heater and wipers on, and raced back to the Birdcage Club where they arrived between 12.20 and 12.30 am.

Witnesses Supporting the Prosecution

In support of their theory, the Crown called an electrical draughtsman and three colliery workers who had reported seeing cars, of the same type, driving in convoy along the A182 that night. Their first witness was Joseph Knight, a draughtsman living at Garden Terrace in Thornley. That night he was driving home from work, along the A182, leaving Houghton-Le-Spring at about 11.30 p.m. As he reached the junction with the B1284, at Fencehouses, he noticed two vehicles. Examined by Mr Castle-Miller, for the Prosecution, he told the court: 'When I was approaching this junction…and was about fifty yards away and there was two cars pulled out in front of us.'
'Were you able to recognize the makes of the two cars?'
'Well, I thought at the time that the first one was an E-Type Jaguar and I was sure that the second one was a Mark X Jaguar.'
'Did you happen to notice any part of the registration plate or number of the Mark X?'
'I did notice that it was a registration which ended with a D'.

'Did the Mark X present its back to you as it drove off…and was it on the back number-plate you thought you saw the letter D?'
'I did see it, yes.'
'What sort of speed were they making?'
'Just below thirty.'
'How close were they driving? How close was the front of the Mark X to the back of the E-Type?'
'They were very close. I would not like to say because being behind them I could not ascertain this very well.'
'Did you wait for them to come out across your bows?'
'Oh, no. They came out as I was approaching'.
'Over what distance did you follow them?'
'Approximately half a mile'.
'How close were you to the Mark X?'
'Just two or three yards.'
'Did you later overtake them?'
'Yes. It was a point at a place near the Picture House called the 'Cosy' in Easington Lane where the road widens'.
'And when you came to a junction called the Snippersgate, which way did you turn?'
'I turned right onto the B1280 to Haswell.'
'Did you ever see those two vehicles again?'
'Only after I turned around. For curiosity's sake I looked in my rear-view mirror to see if, in fact, the first car was an E-Type Jaguar because I had not been too sure prior to that time'.

A few minutes before Joseph Knight began his drive home, colliery overman, Henry Johnson, left South Hetton colliery and walked to the main road, turning right to go to a bus shelter a short distance down the road. Henry Scott asked him:
'Did you notice anything as you were standing there waiting for your bus?'
'I noticed two cars pass me. The first one was a red E-Type Jaguar and the second was a dark coloured Jaguar saloon.'
'What time would that be, Mr Johnson?'
'Fourteen minutes to twelve, midnight.'
'How do you know that; it is a rather exact time?'
'After they passed me, I looked at my watch to see what time it was for my bus.'
'How fast were these cars going?'
'Between twenty-five and thirty miles an hour.'
'How far apart were they?'
'No more than five yards.'
'Could you see how many people there were in them?
'There was one person in the first car, the E-Type and there was two in the saloon.'

This part of the road is illuminated by sodium lamps, but Henry Johnson insisted the unnatural lighting had not confused him. He was quite certain that the E-Type was red, although he didn't know at all the colour of the second vehicle.

On this it should be pointed out that seeing how many people were in a low slung car like the E-Type, especially at night with the only light coming from overhead sodium lights is by no means easy, and the photograph taken for the police under the same condition shows.

Finishing work on the same shift as Henry Johnson was William Sanderson, an engine man. He too left the colliery about 11.45 and walked with his friend, William Cook, down the road towards Easington. He told the court that, as they passed the Bridge Inn, some twenty yards from Pesspool Bridge:

'Two cars passed us travelling in the same direction as us, towards Easington. The first one was an E-Type Jaguar and the second one was a large Jaguar saloon.'

'Are you able to tell the court what the colour of either of these cars was?' Castle-Miller asked.

'The first one as it went under the light on the south side of the bridge, I noticed was a reddish colour, but the second was a dark colour and I couldn't say what colour it was.'

He estimated the cars were travelling no more than five or six yards apart and their speed was not more than thirty mph.

The fourth witness for the prosecution was James Golden, a young miner who initially told the police he left the colliery at 11.40 to cycle home along the A182 to Easington. His evidence is so vital and, although the prosecution seemed unaware of it during the trial, so devastating to the Crown's case we will detail with it in detail in Chapter Twelve. One important point to note here is that he made a total of three statements, to officers of increasing rank, altering his departure time between the first and second to better suit the police version of the murder.

Evidence that the collision and murder had taken place on the A182, opposite West Moor Farm, fell into three categories. As we have already noted, farmer's wife Nora Burnip, heard two sharp cracks shortly after switching off her light to go to sleep. Five cartridge cases, Sibbet's spectacles and fragments of broken Perspex and glass were found at this point.

To establish that it was these two particular cars which had been in collision and caused the debris to be left both here and in Pesspool Lane, the prosecution called automobile expert Mr Stanley Denton, a Senior Experimental Officer at the Northern Forensic Laboratories. His evidence is so complicated and so crucial that it will be dealt with fully in a later chapter. For the moment it is sufficient to say that he concluded that the two cars had collided opposite West Moor Farm.

If the prosecution theory is right, Stafford and Luvaglio must have carried out the murder against an extremely tight schedule. They would have had little more than four minutes to shoot Sibbet, drag his lifeless body across a muddy verge, heave him into the back of the Mark X, drive to Pesspool Lane, clean out the vehicles and abandon the saloon. They then had to drive thirty miles, part of it along a winding country lane, to arrive at the Birdcage Club between 12.20 and 12.30 am.

The Police Conduct a Test Drive
The police felt confident they had established that all this could be completed in the time available and conducted a test drive to prove their point. Detective Superintendent Arthur Chapman, who with Detective Superintendent Collinson carried out the test, was asked by Henry Scott:

'Starting from the Four Lane Ends at Hetton-Le-Hole, that is the junction of the B1284 and the A182, did you start a journey in a Mark X Jaguar?'
'Yes, Sir.'
'And did you travel via Easington Lane, South Hetton, Pesspool Bridge, the A182 road, Pesspool Lane, Haswell, and back to Pesspool Bridge, South Hetton?'
'Yes, Sir.'
'Where did you stop the first time?'
'I stopped at a point along the A182 road, indicated by Superintendent Collinson?'
'How long did you stop there for?'
'Four minutes.'
'Did you then drive on to Pesspool Lane and did you stop there?'
'Yes, Sir, for three minutes.'
    Collinson went on to describe how he and his colleague had returned to Pesspool Bridge where they stopped for about two minutes. They then turned the car around and travelled via South Hetton to the Birdcage Club in Newcastle. They had started their test drive at eleven forty-four and thirty seconds and arrived at the Birdcage Club about twelve thirty-one. He said that they had never exceeded more than seventy mph. along the de-restricted parts of the road and obeyed speed limits when in force.
    It was a fine night when they did the journey, on Saturday 4 March (three days before the trial started) and the road conditions were excellent. As we have seen, three months earlier on the night of the murder road conditions were very different, with ice and strong snow flurries. The characteristics of the E-Type meant it would have been a far more difficult vehicle to handle, at speed, under the road conditions of January 5 than the far heavier saloon. Furthermore, according to the police's own version of events they must have driven around in a circle in order to return to South Hetton and dumped the

Mark X near Pesspool Bridge before retracing their previous root along Pesspool Lane to re-join the A182 north of the village.

It is clear from the evidence of Mr Joseph Knight, who first saw the two cars at approximately 11.35, that Stafford and Luvaglio must have left Peterlee well before the time they claimed. If the prosecution theory is to be tenable it had to 11.30 at the latest. What then are the facts surrounding their departure from Westmorland Rise on the night of January 4?

Leaving Westmoreland Rise

The Crown called three witnesses, two of them police officers and the third a neighbour of Stafford's, George Wells, to give evidence about the time they left. Mr Wells, whose home overlooked the rear of Stafford's house and garage, recalled seeing the E-Type, parked in front of Selena Jones's Mercedes, being turned around. Mr Henry Scott asked him:

'What time was it that you saw the E-Type turned around?'

'About eleven.'

'Did you see who was driving it?'

'No, Sir.'

'At the time it was being driven did you see Mr Stafford at all?'

'In his own drive, yes.'

'Did you see whether or not he got into the E-Type?'

'No.'

'And the last you saw; it was driven away down Westmorland Rise?'

'Yes, Sir.'

'Of course, it is the only way it could go to get out?'

'Yes, Sir.'

In view of the above exchange it is hardly surprising that Raymond Lyons rose indignantly to his feet and protested: 'My Lord, my learned friend is leading.'

To which Mr Justice O'Connor replied, 'Quite right Mr Lyons.'

'And it maybe he was wrongly leading.'

'Well, maybe.'

Henry Scott appeared equally indignant at this suggestion, commenting irritably: 'I don't know what the problem is.'

The defence counsel's objection became clear with his first question in cross-examination: 'Did you actually see the car driven away?'

'No, Sir.'

'You started by saying that when you first saw Mr Stafford that night it was eleven or after, is that right?

'Yes.'

'Is this the position, that you cannot be precise about the time?

'Cannot be, no.'

'Do you remember, after giving evidence at the Committal proceedings going

and discussing the question of time with a Miss Jones?'
'I never did, no.'
'Did you ever say to a her, that it might have been half-past eleven?'
'Yes, I can remember saying that. Yes, it may have been later.'
'What matters really, is this. Might it have been half past eleven when the car was driven away?'
'It could have been.'
'Or perhaps just after?'
'Well, there is two times stick in my head, that is five past eleven and twenty-five to twelve. They are the times I noticed the clock, but I cannot tell you exactly when the car left in between them times.'
'What you mean is, it was either five past eleven or twenty-five to twelve or in between?'
'Well, it could have been in between. I am not sure exactly when it left.'
'Just help us,' instructed Mr Justice O'Connor. 'For some reason you have five past eleven and twenty-five to twelve in your mind?
'Yes, Sir.'
'Would you tell us what the reason is?'
'At five past eleven I put the alarm clock on for the following morning and at twenty-five to twelve I started shouting at my wife for staying in the bath so long.'
'And all this, seeing Mr Stafford and the car go up the road, turn around and stop, happened between those two things?'
'Yes'.
'The real position is that you have no idea when between those two times it was?' said Mr Lyons.
'I have not, no.'
'It could have been as late as twenty-five to twelve?'
'Yes, Sir.'

We have already described the evidence of the other two witnesses, police officers Kell and Mitchell, who both stated, on oath, that during their first interview with Dennis Stafford and Michael Luvaglio the accused had said they left Peterlee at eleven o'clock. This the two men strongly deny, a denial which seems to be supported by George Wells' evidence.

There can, at least, be little doubt that Stafford and Luvaglio arrived at the Birdcage night club between 12.20 and 12.30. There is the evidence of the doorman Matthew Dean, the entertainers Allen and McGarry, and to a lesser extent the club's manager Mr Bowden. During their test run the police assumed that Stafford and Luvaglio had abandoned the Mark X at Pesspool Bridge about 12.07 before racing back to Newcastle, arriving at 12.31. What evidence did the prosecution call to support their contention?

Three men had driven along the A182 between 12.30 and 1 am. The first was Mr Sidney Lee, a farmer, who was on his way to Easington Village when, at 12.35, he drove under Pesspool Bridge. He told the court that he saw a car parked there but nobody in or near it. He thought that the lights were on.

Mr Clifford Miller, the second witness, a van driver living in West Hartlepool, was driving along the same route at 12.45 and confirmed Mr Lee's observation. He had noticed the vehicle's sidelights were on and the driver's window was open.

The last of the witnesses was Reuben Conroy, a livestock transporter, who had been travelling in the opposite direction to the others, from Easington towards Easington Lane. He arrived at the bridge at about 12.50 am and noticed the Mark X parked there, its sidelights were on and windscreen wipers working. He could not say whether or not the vehicle was damaged. Mr Henry Scott asked him: 'Was there anything which drew your attention to it?' 'Just the position that it was standing. It seemed to be in a bad patch of the road, you know.'

According to the same police timetable of events, Sibbet was shot at about 11.50 am. Under cross-examination, Detective Superintendent Arthur Chapman told the court how, during the test drive, he and his colleague had arrived at the alleged murder scene at 11.50 and 30 seconds and left at precisely 11.54 and 30 seconds.

'Allowing four minutes for the commission of the offence?' Raymond Dean suggested.

'I do not agree that I allowed four minutes for the commission of the offence,' Chapman objected. 'I stopped there for four minutes.'

'This is the time you allowed on your journey, assuming the man had been pulled out of the car and shot on that spot?' enquired the judge.

'And put back again?' added Raymond Dean.

'Yes, Sir,' Chapman said. 'I accept that.'

How Angus Sibbet Died

For the prosecution's theory to be correct, Sibbet must have been shot within a very few minutes of this estimated time. The medical evidence as to time of death was, therefore, vital. This was provided by Dr Jack Eric Ennis, the police pathologist, who was asked by Mr Scott:

'Could you, from what you found on the body and in the body, assess the probable time of death?'

'Within a fairly wide range, yes.'

'What is your range?'

'From midnight until four o'clock in the morning. But it is much more likely that death occurred in the earlier part of that period. I would say between twelve and one o'clock. Twelve midnight and one o'clock.'

As we explained in the previous chapter, the post-mortem examination, and tests carried out on Sibbet's clothing by forensic scientific and ballistic experts, showed three shots had been fired into the victim at very close range. The fatal bullet entered from behind, penetrating down through the left shoulder and severing one of the major blood vessels from the heart. It was common ground that these shots occurred in rapid succession and Sibbet had died within sixty seconds, as evidenced by the lack of bleeding.

The prosecution alleged that, after the collision, the driver of the E-Type had run back to the saloon just as Sibbet was getting out. The killer produced an automatic and fired five times. Despite the point-blank range, two shots went wide. One shattered the rear off-side window of the Mark X, and another struck the door stay. In the witness box Dr Ennis felt able to give the court a 'simple and straightforward explanation' of how these injuries had been inflicted:

'I visualise that the deceased had opened the car door and was emerging, holding the door still with his left hand and his right hand somewhat against the right hand side of the abutment and the first injury he would then receive was the one which passed through the right, lower, forearm and through the right loin tissues. I visualise, then, that he ducked and, in the course, of ducking and stooping down, he then received a second wound, probably the one on the left, behind the left shoulder followed very quickly by the third one on the right lower chest. He then falls forward onto his face and onto his hands and the front part of his body.'

Dr Ennis agreed this was only speculation and that Sibbet could have been shot in other ways. Mr Lyons challenged this reconstruction and offered an alternative theory which Dr Ennis declined to accept. In our view exactly how, the murder was actually committed, in what order the shots were fired, and the relative positions of victim and gunman when they the killing occurred, are of no real importance when considering the guilt or innocence of Stafford and Luvaglio.

We have sought to present prosecution's case in the strongest possible light. While, at first sight, it may appear reasonably plausible and straightforward, in the next chapter we will describe the many anomalies and inconsistencies it contains.

Chapter Nine: When Did Angus Sibbet Die?

'Cooling of the body is the most important early phenomenon in the estimation of the time of death and every factor in connection therewith must be recorded and carefully considered.' Pathologist Keith Simpson.

For Dennis and Michael to have killed their apparent friend and colleague, Angus had to be shot between eleven and midnight. Outside that, very narrow, time frame both men had, as we have shown, incontestable alibis. For this reason, medical evidence relating to time of death was of paramount importance. Let's take a detailed look at this evidence to see how accurate and reliable it actually was.

The corpse of Angus Stuart Sibbet was found at 5.15 am. Police were on the scene by 5.30 and pathologist Dr Jack Ennis arrived at 8.05 am. Yet he did not begin the post-mortem until 1.15 that afternoon. In the witness box Dr Ennis was asked, by Rudolph Lyons, about the likely consequence of this eight-hour delay:

'The car, we have been told, was not removed until nine o'clock?'
'Yes.'
'But you did not take the temperature of the body at nine o'clock, did you?'
'No.'
'You waited until the afternoon at quarter past one?'
'Yes.'
'Which makes it more difficult to come to a reliable estimate of the time of death?'
'It does, yes.'

As we have explained, the police theory required that Stafford and Luvaglio had shot Sibbet within minutes of 11.50 pm. No earlier, or later time was possible. Even if the medical evidence about time of death had been more accurate, it still wouldn't have made a significant difference to the prosecution case. If, for example, Ennis had established Sibbet had died between, say 11.30 pm and 12.30 am, while doing nothing to discredit the evidence of the defendants, would at least make the prosecution case, at least in this respect, possible. If, however, death had occurred between 12.30 and 1.30 am, the entire prosecution theory would collapse.

With every minute that passed the body temperature was falling, reducing, as Dr Ennis agreed in court, the accuracy of any estimate. As the pathologists' bible, of the day, *Taylor's Medical Jurisprudence*, says: 'Cooling of the body is the most important early phenomenon in the estimation of time of death and every factor in connection therewith must be recorded and carefully considered'.

When a pathologist examines a corpse, in order to determine time of death, the main factors, she or he looks for are rigor mortis, hypostasis - the pooling of blood under the skin causing lividity - and cooling. Other more minor

76

post-mortem change, such as an analysis of stomach content, are also sometimes helpful. There is no simple formula whereby the rate of cooling can be determined precisely, though there are a number of things which affect a corpse's loss of heat. The primary factor is the difference in temperature between the body and the surroundings. Generally, the greater the difference, the more rapid is the rate of loss, and the build of the deceased must be considered since fat is a poor conductor of heat.

No less important is the clothing and surrounding temperature. Of this *Taylor's Medical Jurisprudence* notes: 'A body in air loses heat by convection and radiation; some, however, will be lost by conduction through the material on which the body is lying. Anything which will increase the rate of radiation, conduction, or convection will accelerate cooling.' A body lying exposed in a well-ventilated space, for example, will cool more rapidly than one in a sealed room, as the freely circulating air will rapidly carry away that warmed by the body.

What factors here would have influenced the rate of cooling?

Sibbet's weight was estimated (never accurately weighed), by Dr Ennis, at fourteen stone. He was wearing vest and pants, shirt, suit, and a shortie overcoat, though coat and jacket were pulled up and wide open when his body was found. Since it is the prosecution theory Dr Ennis was supporting, let us consider his evidence in relation to the events the police allege occurred that night.

According to Jack Ennis, of the three shots fired into his body the one passing through the left shoulder and penetrating the heart was fatal. Rudolph Lyons asked him: 'After that bullet wound had done its work, how long would life last in the body?' To which he replied:
'Not more than a minute.'

This means that cooling began immediately, according to the police theory, before midnight. The body was dumped in the back of the saloon whose rear off-side window, again according to the prosecution, had already been shot out. The car was then driven a few hundred yards to Pesspool Lane where it has been suggested the body was thrown out again to account for the mud staining on the clothing, although this may have occurred as Sibbet fell to the ground after being shot. In any event by midnight his clothes were stained with wet mud and the evaporation of moisture alone would help accelerate the cooling. The car, after being driven a few miles, was abandoned near the bridge, but not sufficiently beneath it to gain any shelter. By this time, it appears the driver's window was also open (from the evidence of miner Clifford Miller) and it was certainly open when the body was found.

All the witnesses confirm that there were snow flurries throughout the period, and a fairly strong north-westerly wind was blowing. The air temperature. recorded by Dr Ennis at 8.05 a.m. was 26°F, and it seems likely that the body had been in a temperature of below freezing since before midnight. Even after being transferred to the mortuary the temperature only rose to 28°F. Despite the fact that Sibbet was a big man one would expect a fairly rapid rate of cooling. Dr Ennis drew no conclusion from an examination of the stomach contents, and from the hypostasis (pooling of the blood) found only that the body had been resting in the same position since shortly after death.

At 1.15 pm the body was affected by rigor mortis, but the important point is whether rigor was established at 6 am, when Dr Seymour Hunter made his brief examination. Rigor occurs when pumps regulating calcium, stop functioning. Calcium floods the cells causing the muscles to contract and stiffen. It typically sets in three to four hours after death, peaks at 12 hours, and disappears after forty-eight. Dr Hunter told the Peterlee magistrates what he had found:

'On 5 January 1967 I was called by the police to examine a man in a car under Pesspool Bridge. I received the call at 5.40 am. I arrived there ten minutes later. The man in the car was in the position shown in the photograph three of Exhibit Number Two. I examined him as far as possible. He was dead. There was an abrasion, roughly circular, on the forehead towards the right-hand side. There was some soil and grit around the abrased area and the right side of the face. There was no pillow behind the body. The white shown in photograph number three of Exhibit Two is the man's shirt sleeve. His jacket was off the right arm, but I am not sure of the left arm which I could not see as it was hidden under the body. I do not recollect seeing any overcoat. The part of the garment in photograph number three to the right side of the head of the body is either part of the jacket or jacket and overcoat. There was a jacket but whether the man had it on the left sleeve or not I am not sure. I am uncertain whether there was an overcoat at all. There were trousers on the body. I would not like to commit myself as to whether the fly was open or not.'

According to Dr Hunter's evidence, quoted above in full, no test for rigor mortis was made. It appears his brief examination was largely to establish Sibbet was actually dead. At the trial, however, Dr Hunter introduced entirely new evidence as to whether rigor was present.
'Were you able to form an opinion as to whether the man was alive or dead?' he was asked.
'Yes, he was dead.'
'How did you ascertain that?'
'By his general appearance. The pallor. The presence of rigor mortis and the tissues were coagulated.'
'Did you move the body at all?'
'I took hold of the left leg and raised it slightly to ascertain the presence of rigor mortis.'
'And the position of the arm and head, and so on, did you alter them at all?'
'No.'

But was rigor actually established?

In Chapter One we discussed how miner Tom Leak, a man used to making careful observations under challenging conditions, was sure that, when he first saw the body, the left leg it was straight. Photographs taken thirty minutes later, one of which is shown below, after considerable activity at the scene, show it to be bent. Tom Leak was quite certain of what he saw and clearly had no reason to lie. He claims he never altered the position of the leg, but certainly it appears somebody did at some time during the intervening period. Commenting on this, the eminent Home Office pathologist Professor Francis Camps told us: 'There must be some error here, because if the leg was stiff with rigor mortis, it could not have been bent by Leak as once broken down it will not go stiff again.'

Whether Leak, or somebody else, bent the dead man's leg is beside the point. What matters here is that if rigor mortis had been present in the leg at 5.15 am and if, some time before Dr Hunter's examination at 5.50 am, the limb was bent, rigor mortis would have been destroyed and could not have been felt in the left leg. The only limb used by Dr Hunter to test for it.

On the second day of the trial, the plump and balding figure of Dr Jack Ennis stepped into the witness box and was sworn in. As we described, in the previous chapter, he told the court about the events of 5 January, the position of the wounds and how he envisaged they had been inflicted. Following the lunch adjournment, Henry Scott asked him:

'Could you, from what you found on the body and in the body, assess the probable time of death?'

'Within a fairly wide range, yes.'

'And what is your range?'

'From midnight to four o'clock in the morning, but it is much more likely that death occurred in the earlier part of that period. I would say between twelve and one o'clock, twelve midnight and one o'clock.'

'From the position of his body in the car, can you tell whether, when he was put into that car, he was dead?'

'I would say he was dead when he was put into the car.'

'You think he was dead; why do you say that, Dr Ennis?'

'Because of the position in which the body was found, just as though it had been dumped in. He would surely have moved somewhat if he was still alive.'

That was all the court would have heard about the time of death had it not been for the fact that Mr Lyons decided to cross-examine on this point.

'Now I want to ask you about the time. Obviously, it is a very important matter, the determination of the time, if possible?

'Yes.'

'That is done by taking the temperature of the body?'

'Yes, Sir.'

'At the time of your examination, it was, I gather, about 64°F?'

'64°F, yes.'

'You then took that from the normal temperature of 98°F?'
'Yes.'
'So, he has lost thirty-four degrees of heat?'
'Yes.'
'Then you have got to assess how many degrees have been lost per hour, according to the circumstances?'
'Yes.'
'And the conclusion to which you came was somewhere between twelve and four?'
'Yes.'
'Subject to this, that if anything, you prefer twelve to two?'
'Yes, and nearer the beginning of that time.'
'That is one thing I don't understand, perhaps you can explain it. If you say twelve to four but probably twelve to two, one might argue this, more probably one to two than twelve to one. You see you have eliminated up to twelve.
'I have not eliminated it, no, one cannot be absolutely exact when giving time.'
'No?'
'But this is on the various findings. I would say this is the range in which I would place the time of death.'
'You have taken a very wide range of four hours.'
'Yes.'
'Therefore, your opinion at the time you gave it, and you mentioned four hours, is that it was very unlikely it was before or after that period, although anything is possible, is that right?'
'Yes.'
'And if you say, well, of the four hours I prefer the first two, does not that make it more likely that taking two single hours, twelve to one; one to two; it is more likely that it is one to two than twelve to one.'
'No, I prefer...'
'You prefer twelve to one?'
'Yes.'
'Would half past twelve be a reasonable time?'
'Yes.'
'Twenty past twelve?'
'Yes.'
'More probably twenty past twelve or half past twelve than before twelve?'
'I would not argue it could not have occurred a short time before twelve.'
'That is not what I am asking you, we are going on probabilities.'
'We cannot be precise in stating a time.'
'If you had thought that this could have happened by twelve, you would have said eleven thirty to four, or eleven to four?'
'Yes.'
'You said twelve to four, giving yourself a very wide range?'

'Yes.'

'Therefore, it is more probable in your opinion, is it not, that it happened at twelve twenty or twelve thirty than that it happened before twelve?'

'If you wish to pin me down to a time, I would say round about twelve o'clock and no nearer than that.'

'Why didn't you say, originally, between eleven and one, or something like that, if that is your view?'

'Well, for a few reasons. One was the remarkable rate of cooling which has taken place in this particular body, and secondly, I was not aware at the time that I completed my report that, in fact, rigor mortis was confirmed at six o'clock in the morning'.

'You knew that that body had been in a freezing car for hours?'

'Yes.'

'The temperature at eight o'clock in the morning was 26°F, six degrees of frost?'

'Yes.'

'At the time two of the windows were completely open?'

'Yes.'

'It must have been freezing inside the car at eight o'clock in the morning?'

'Yes.'

'It must have been freezing, I mean below 32°F for many hours?'

'Yes, well, no. I would not say for many hours because we don't know how much heat the interior of the car had retained. The heater had been on. That is another thing which I was not aware of at the time.'

'Are you saying that the heater was working at any time you saw it?

'No.'

'Have you any reason to believe the heater was working at, let us say, five o'clock in the morning?'

'Yes.'

'Why do you say that?'

'Because I have since had information that the fan was still - the fan of the heater was still working when the car was first found.'

'When you got there, there was unmelted snow in the car was there not?'

'Yes.'

'And on the man's hair?'

'Yes.'

'We have heard there was unmelted snow at five something in the morning?'

'Yes.'

'At any rate, there was no sign on the outside of the car of any melting caused by internal heat?'

'No, not at the time.'

'The snow is quite solid all around the car, is that correct?'

'Yes.'

'At any rate you came to a conclusion of twelve to four. I just want to know, are you now saying you have changed your mind?

'No. If you asked me to draw a graph of the probability, and the probability in my mind would be highest soon after twelve o'clock and it would tail off towards the latter period. It would come down very steeply indeed.'

'Why then did you not say in your original report eleven to four or eleven to three instead of twelve to four?'

'Because I was not aware that rigor mortis had been tested for at the time, I think it was by Doctor Hunter.'

'That means you have changed your mind.'

Dr Ennis gave the defence counsel a long, hard, stare through the thick lenses of his glasses, before replying defiantly.

'Hardly.'

After asking further questions about why such a long delay had occurred, between the finding of the body and starting the post-mortem, Mr Lyons returned to the perplexing matter of the rate of cooling.

'At what rate do you estimate the body had cooled per hour. How many degrees per hour?'

'If the body had cooled at the rate of 2.6 °F per hour, that is, in thirteen hours, it took me back to about midnight. If, on the other hand, I estimate the rate of cooling at 3°F per hour, that took me back to half past one, but in arriving at a time I had to consider the degree of rigor mortis.'

'Are you familiar with Taylor's jurisprudence book, written by Mr Keith Simpson, on medical jurisprudence?'

'Yes.'

'Do you remember an instance quoted of a body in snow in a temperature of 32°F to 36°F?'

'Yes.'

'Was it not proved in that case that the rate of cooling was 3.6°F an hour.'

'Four degrees, I think, wasn't it? It was four degrees in that particular case.'

'The book says 3.6°F and you picked 2.6°F.'

'I took the lower, yes.'

'The higher the degree of course, the later the time of death?'

'Yes.'

'If you take the average of 3°F. what time would that give you? I am taking the average between the figure that Dr Keith Simpson speaks about for the body in the snow and the figure you actually took.'

'Yes. That would take us to half past one. Now, we cannot compare the particular case recorded there because that was lying in snow from the beginning. In this case the body was in a car which must have been warm for the first part of the cooling period.'

'Just ignoring the question of the heater for the moment, would you agree that without a heater, even if the car had been warm to start with, with two windows out and a temperature of 26°F, it would have been under 32'F within an hour

inside of that car?'
'I was not aware that both windows were out.'
'I think that is the evidence.'
'Only one.'
'One fully open, the other shattered out completely, but two completely open windows.'
'As far as I understood the window was wound down.'
'Does that make any difference, whether it was wound down or knocked out, for this purpose?'
'No, the driver's window was wound down by somebody after the car had been found.'
'I don't think that is the evidence.'
'I might be open to correction.'
'Were you estimating that was the position in coming to your figure of 2.6°F?'
'No, no.'
'Would you assume for the moment that two windows were, for different reasons, completely open.'
'Yes.'
'From sometime early in that morning at any rate. Do you agree that within an hour of that happening the temperature inside that car, subject to any heater, must have been below freezing?'
'It would, yes it would be.'
        Mr Justice O'Connor interjected: 'It depends when the temperature outside fell to freezing point.'
'Yes, My Lord.' Dr Ennis agreed.
'Do you know?'
'We don't know. My Lord. These are the variables here.'
'We know there were flurries of snow during the night,' Rudolph Lyons pointed out, 'so the temperature could not have been so much above freezing point. Do you agree?'
'Yes, I agree that.'
'There are, of course, other ways, are there not, of forming a judgement about the time of death?'
'May we just go back again to the temperature within the car. You will recall that the heater was still functioning... That is yet another of the peculiar weather conditions or peculiar air conditions in the car.'
'If the engine is not running does the heater blow hot air or cold air?'
'This again is another factor. For the latter half of the period I am sure that cold air was being blown onto the body.'
'How long do you think that hot air would come in from the heater once the car is stationary in these particular conditions that night, half an hour?'
'At least half an hour.'
        We have cited this lengthy transcript due to the importance of Dr

Ennis's evidence and because each of his answers needs to be considered in relation to the testimony as a whole.

He chose a cooling rate which was low. Low by comparison with the similar case quoted in *Taylor's Medical Jurisprudence*. Low by comparison with an estimate subsequently made by Professor Francis Camps. Rudolph Lyons suggested to Dr Ennis that a 3°F per hour cooling rate was reasonable. Accepting this tiny 0.4° F difference, the time of Sibbet's death becomes two o'clock (not one thirty as Dr Ennis calculated from the witness box). In which case Stafford and Luvaglio could not have committed the murder.

Only if we accept Dr Ennis's reasons for choosing the lower rate, and agree that this is probable, does the police theory still hold. It was clearly a difficult job for any pathologist to make a completely fair calculation based solely on the evidence, rather than the mass of speculation which surrounded it. But the only facts which Dr Ennis should fairly have considered were that that the car was found with Sibbet's body in it at 5.15 am, with both off side windows wide open, the heater fan switched on, snow on Sibbet's clothes and hair, together with the fact his clothes were stained with wet mud and his jacket open. He had also to consider that the temperature outside at eight o'clock in the morning was 26°F, that the body was kept in sub-zero conditions up to the time he took a rectal temperature. There had been heavy snow flurries throughout the night, and snow had settled over the car by 5.15.

These were the basic facts and it is interesting to see how many of them he had actually taken into account.

Firstly, he was certain that the driver's window was closed until after 5.15. When told he was wrong, he denied it would have made any difference to his calculations.

He agreed it was freezing inside the car at 8 am but would not agree that this had been the position for many hours: 'I would not say for many hours because we don't know how much heat the interior of the car had retained.'

He assumed the heater had been blowing hot air over the body for at least half an hour, and cold air for only the latter part of the period. This suggests that, in his opinion, the air inside the Mark X had been warm, for between two and four hours. Here again Dr Ennis is open to correction. And corrected he was, by another prosecution witness, Mr Sunter, the Jaguar car expert, during this exchange with Mr Castle-Miller:
'Will you imagine that the engine is not running but the ignition is switched on?'
'Yes.'
'And the water has drained out through the hole you found…How long would anything like warm air be drawn through the heater system?'
'A minute.'

Dr Ennis believed only one window was open and that for the first part of the period, variously estimated, warm or hot air was being blown over the corpse. On both he was in wrong. It would also have been useful for him to have found the night air temperature; Angus Sibbet's precise weight and what tests had been made for rigor mortis.

From the transcript quoted above it can be seen that under cross-examination Dr Ennis changed his time estimate despite no new evidence having been presented to him. At the start of his testimony, for example, he states in reply to a question about his time range: 'The wide range from midnight to four a.m. But it is much more likely that death occurred in the earlier part of that period. I would say between twelve and one o'clock.'

As he came to the end of his testimony Mr Justice O'Connor asked him:

'Doctor, if rigor mortis was found established at six o'clock in the morning, if you had known that at the time of your first report, would you have, on the temperature chart, would you have taken a bracket of twelve to four?'

'No, my Lord.'

'What bracket would you have taken?'

'Er ... probably from about eleven to two.'

It is difficult to see how Dr Ennis could honestly hold the first opinion if he also believed the second. When he took the oath, he was aware of the evidence as to rigor mortis, such as it was, and had the opportunity of revising his opinion before he came to give evidence. Yet he persisted in saying that his time bracket was twelve to four, when, according to his later testimony, he really believed the bracket was eleven to two. It was certainly not a slip of the tongue, he stuck by this time bracket - as can be seen from the transcript - through question after question. It was suggested to him, as we have seen, that he was changing his mind, and his retort was: 'Hardly.'

Defence produced no expert evidence to comment on or contradict the estimate and certainly we are not qualified to do so. Subsequent to the trial we sought the opinion of Professor Francis Camps, an internationally acclaimed criminal pathologist. The report, on the body's cooling rate, he prepared at our request states: 'As a result of reference I have made to data which has been presented by forensic pathologists and on the basis of my own experience, the margin of time of death, under conditions reasonably approximating to those revealed by the evidence, falls between a minimum of 10 1/2 hours and a maximum of 13 1.2 hours, which places the time of death, in this case, between 11.45 p.m. and 2.45 a.m., accounting for a drop between 2.6°F and 3.2°F per hour. This calculation is based on a normal rectal temperature of 99°F as opposed to 98.4°F. There is no justification for choosing, as between these terminal figures the lower figure in preference to any other. The mean figure would place the time of death at 1.30 a.m.'

Before leaving the subject of the cooling rate and the factors surrounding it, we must point out that in a later chapter we introduce evidence, not presented at the trial, which suggests that the windows of the Mark X were still all intact and closed at about 2.30 am. If Sibbet was dead and lying in the vehicle, though we shall also introduce evidence to suggest he may still have been alive as late as 12.45 am, and the windows were closed and unbroken for some of the night, then it could be argued that Dr Ennis's estimate becomes slightly more probable. But in that case the prosecution theory is, of course, entirely wrong.

Looking at the events of that night through the eyes of the prosecution we see a collision at speed; fragments of broken glass and Perspex - from seven light units – flakes of red and green paint littering the scene; Sibbet shot three times at point blank range; two more shots fired into his car, one of them spraying shattered Triplex over the back seat and floor of the Mark X. Sibbet's body, lying face down on the road, is dragged with desperate urgency onto the muddy grass at the side of the road so that his clothes became heavily stained, down to the vest. The muddy, bleeding corpse is then manhandled into the back of the car. One of the accused drives for a few hundred yards, stopping to clean it out, before continuing on to Pesspool Bridge. All this taking place on a black night well away from any artificial lighting.

That, in summary, is the prosecution theory. As we explained, in Chapter Four, when Stafford and Luvaglio strolled into the Birdcage Club they appeared spotlessly clean. There is, of course, all the difference in the world between a casual observation and the rigorous examinations, including chemical and microscopic testing, which modern science has placed at the disposal of the forensic experts.

Altogether sixty-two items of Stafford's clothing and eleven of Luvaglio's were sent to Mr Norman Lee at the Northern Forensic Laboratories, as were samples of soil, grass, paint, Perspex, fragments of glass and vacuum sweepings from inside both vehicles. Three of Stafford's suits had been collected from the Zip Cleaners, by Detective Constable Richardson, and these too were handed to Mr Lee.

After a most careful and detailed examination of all this clothing, he was only able to find about a dozen red paint fragments, some 1/25th an inch in diameter in the jacket of a grey pinstripe suit belonging to Stafford, and two more in the trouser pockets. These were in one of the suits recovered from the Zip Cleaners and therefore one of those placed in the boot of the E-Type on 6 January by Dennis Stafford shortly after he had examined the extent of the damage. His explanation was that these paint chips had probably been transferred from the car to the suit at that time. In the witness box, Detective Sergeant Morgan not only agreed was perfectly possible but added that, in his experience, it was usual. Mr Lyons asked him:

'Would it surprise you if, on very careful examination of one of your pockets of that suit, some chips of paint were found in it, minute chips?'

'I would expect them to be found.'

'Why would you expect them to be found?'

'Because I was handling the red E-Type Jaguar yesterday'.

It is only fair to say that Mr Norman Lee did not share this view although he confirmed that literally dozens of foreign fibres would often be found in a pocket.

It was the unchallenged evidence of Stafford that he was wearing the same suit when he went to Peterlee police station as he had worn the night before. This too was carefully examined by Mr Lee, who was questioned on his findings by Mr Lyons:

'Did you find any grass debris on the clothing of Mr Stafford?'
'No, Sir.'
'Or of Mr Luvaglio?'
'No, Sir.'
'You examined quite a number of pairs of shoes of Mr Stafford?'
'Yes.'
'Did you find any on his shoes?'
'No, Sir.'
'The ladies on the jury will know how easy it is to carry grass debris onto the carpet of a room in the house. Grass debris could be carried by a shoe anywhere?'
'Yes, it could.'
'And deposited by that shoe?'
'Yes.'
'Did you find any grass debris in the E-Type Jaguar?'
'No, Sir.'

The Newcastle Journal, of Friday 17 February, reported the second day of the committal proceedings before Peterlee magistrates under the headline 'Forensic Man Tells of Matching Bloodstains' and the story continued : 'Traces of human blood were found on the interior waistband of a pair of trousers belonging to Michael Luvaglio ... the court heard that forensic experts had identified the stains as belonging to blood group A, the same classification as given to Angus Sibbet, the dead man.'

Anybody who had followed the case from the committal proceedings must have gathered from this that a conclusive link had been found between the accused and their victim.

The true position was very different.

At the trial Mr Lee confirmed that tiny specks of Group A blood had indeed been found on the inner waistband of trousers belonging to Michael Luvaglio. He told Mr Dean: 'It was not a bloodstain so much as a little group of tiny stains.'

So small was the amount of blood found that it could only be generally classified as Group A, which is common to nearly half the population including Angus Sibbet. As Mr Dean pointed out: 'It hardly needs me to say this, but when the trousers have been worn presumably it is the part of the trousers which would be in contact with the shirt or whatever was immediately below?'

'Yes.'

'Not the sort of place where one would likely get a splash of blood if one were wearing the trousers and they were fastened?'

'A most unlikely place.'

A vomit-type stain was found on the inside lower left front on a blue raincoat belonging to Michael Luvaglio. Mr Lee obtained a positive reaction when he tested this stain for blood but was unable to say whether it was actually blood or not, or of course form an opinion as to the Group. As he told the court: 'I am pretty certain it is neither here nor there.'

In the right-side pocket of a pair of check trousers, belonging to Dennis Stafford, an apparently old blood stain was found and classified as Group A. Was it, Mr Lyons wondered, in any way connected with the alleged events of the night of the 4 – 5 January?

'I think it is highly improbable, Sir.' Norman Lee told him.

Finally, on the cuff of a shirt, belonging to Dennis Stafford and recovered from the Zip Cleaners, was found the 'merest trace of apparent blood and the dirt on the cuff (which) appeared to have been wet'.

Lee wasn't asked about this by the prosecution, but Mr Lyons raised the point in his cross-examination:

'Is it the merest trace?'

'No more than the merest trace.'

'No more than the merest trace. In saying that you are strengthening what I am putting to you.'

'And only just the merest trace, exactly.'

'Could you group it?' enquired Mr Justice O'Connor.

'I could not do anything with it.'

'It might be anybody's?' suggested Rudolph Lyons.

'It may not even be human, Sir.

'So that really there is no blood which anybody can reasonably rely upon to link Mr Stafford with this murder? You agree with that?'

'Yes.'

As we have explained, Norman Lee examined every article of clothing belonging to all three men. Studied sweepings and samples from both cars. Although clearly expecting to find a link between Sibbet and the accused, he had been unable to do so, and was perfectly willing to acknowledge it. Since this was the prosecution case and clearly there had been a most thorough investigation it seems strange that Mr Justice O'Connor should have felt the need, at this stage, to qualify his expert evidence by adding: 'Well, not as far as you are aware?'

As we have already seen, the three shots fired entered the upper part of Sibbet's body; one smashed his right wrist and the fatal shot entered his left shoulder. When the heavy corpse was heaved into the car somebody must have grasped him either by the arms or by the shoulders. Fumbling urgently in pitch darkness, it would hardly have been possible to pick and choose the areas free of blood, so how can it be believed that no blood at all was transferred?

Indeed, if the prosecution theory is right it controverts the well-established theory of interchange. In his book, *Final Diagnosis*, Professor John Glaister, an internationally recognised forensic expert with over forty years' experience, deals at length with this theory, of which he says: 'In simple terms it is almost impossible for anyone to go to the scene of a crime without either leaving some trace of his visit behind him or carrying away, all unsuspectingly, some trace which links him with the place.'

The only way there could have been no interchange, if the police theory was correct, would have been for the two accused to have destroyed every item of clothing, including their shoes, at some unspecified time after their return home to Westmorland Rise and before their arrest. The police must have investigated this possibility with the greatest care, but there was never any suggestion from them that this could have happened.

Further as we have said it was the unchallenged evidence of both men that the clothes they were wearing when they went to Peterlee police station were those, they had worn the previous evening. The detectives must, surely, have checked the truth of these statements by questioning everybody who saw them on the night of the murder. In any event, as we have already seen, on arrival at the Birdcage the two men appeared spotlessly clean and immaculately dressed. There was neither the time, nor the opportunity, as they raced back to Newcastle, to even wash their hands.

Not only that, but the theory of interchange works both ways. No evidence was found, either in the Mark X or on Sibbet's clothing and body, to link them to Dennis and Michael. In *Taylor's Medical Jurisprudence* the author has this to say about the quality of evidence: 'In order to convict an accused person on circumstantial evidence, the facts proved in the case should be consistent with his guilt, and be utterly inconsistent with his innocence ... the facts should be such as to render it impossible in the minds of the jury that anyone but the accused could have committed the crime.'

We leave it you to decide how far the evidence detailed in this chapter, and indeed any of the evidence produced in support of the prosecution's case, meets this perfectly reasonable standard.

Chapter Ten: Silent Witnesses

'I disagree with many individual propositions of the prosecution and with the conclusions which they have drawn regarding the damage to the two cars.'
George Bowman, Consultant Engineer.

Evidence of a collision between the E-Type and the Mark X, on the night of January 4, was the cornerstone of the prosecution theory. The only link police could find between Stafford, Luvaglio and the murder scene. These silent witnesses proved sufficient, despite almost overwhelming contradictory evidence, to send the two accused to prison for life.

Their argument was as follows. The accused were driving the sports car. Angus Sibbet's corpse was found in the Mark X. Since the vehicles collided with one another it must follow that only they could have shot dead the fruit machine collector. In a welter of confusion and complexities involved in the case jury members must have felt that here was an unchallengeable piece of evidence. A clear and steady light to guide them, through a dense fog of conflicting testimony, to the truth.

At the trial the defence were unable to offer any evidence to cast doubt on the simple fact that a collision had taken place. Nor could they offer any explanation for the damage apparently linking the vehicles. Before we can accept this, seemingly persuasive, theory however, four vital questions have to be answered:

When did the two vehicles collide?
How many times did they collide?
Were Dennis and Michael driving the E-Type at the time they collided?
Who was most likely to gain from the death of Angus Sibbet?

As we will demonstrate, answering these questions was by no means a simple matter of a dent on one car precisely matching some part of the other vehicle.

The Evidence of Stanley Denton

At ten o'clock the following morning he went to Roker Car Sprays, East Wickham Street, Sunderland, and later the same day examined the red E-Type at Peterlee police station. In his report he stated:' The vehicle was generally in good condition but was damaged at the rear end. 'The off side of the rear number-plate and the rear of the off-side bumper bar had been pushed forward and buckled. The chrome surround of the number-plate recess had been buckled and partly displaced. The rear off-side panel was dented in two places, most probably being caused by impact to the rear of the vehicle. There was a large dent below the off-side rear bumper immediately below the rear light. Both rear lights were devoid of their plastic lenses with the exception of small portions surrounding the securing screws, and in the case of the off-side lens a small sliver of amber plastic in the lower rim. The reversing light cover was

The Mark X as miner Tom Leak found it at 5.15am on January 5, 1967.
The car is facing south down the A182 main road through the village.

The body of Angus Sibbet slumped on the rear seat of his damaged Mark X. The off-side rear window has been shot out and the driver window wound down. Photograph taken not at the scene but some hours later in the yard behind Peterlee police station.

The Luvaglio family reunited after the end of the war. Francis and Maude with Michael, 8 and Vince, 13.
(Michael Luvaglio Family Album)

Vince Luvaglio (later Landa) at the age of eighteen.
(Michael Luvaglio Family Album)

Michael (2nd row from the top, ninth in) with his RAF intake during National Service
(Media-Arts)

Vince with the Kray Twins.
Left to right: Reggie Kray, Vince, Barnie Beal
professional boxer, Bert Battles and
Ronnie Kray
(Photographer Unknown).

Above: Dryderdale Hall where
Vince played Lord of the Manor
(Michael Luvaglio Family Album)

Left: Reggie (third on the left) and Ronnie Kray (first
on the right) with friends, including American singer
Billy Daniels (second from the left) at La Dolce Vita.
(Photographer unknown)

From the left Gwen Landa, Pat Burgess, unknown woman, Vince Landa, Michael Luvaglio and Dennis Stafford, taken during the brothers' first meeting with Dennis at London's Talk of the Town. The man with his back to the camera at the extreme right is MP Reader Harris
(Michael Luvaglio Family Album)

Advertisement for the Bally electrical-mechanical fruit machine favoured by Vince Landa

Dennis Stafford in 1967
(Dennis Stafford collection)

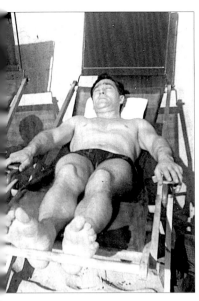

Dartmoor Prison from which Dennis escaped by scaling the wall with fellow inmate William Day (David Lewis archive)

Dennis sunning himself in Trinidad after escaping from England (Dennis Stafford collection)

Superintendent Ronald Kell in the Seventies (Photographer Unknown)

Aerial view of South Hetton showing the key landmarks, named. The colliery is on the left of the picture with the A182, passing under Pesspool Bridge, to its right. West Moor Farm is in the right upper quarter, while the junction with Pesspool Lane can be seen, top right. (Wilson and Cowan, Sunderland).

Close-up of Mark X front shelf showing box of Bahama Cigars.
(Durham Police)

Above: The next police photo still shows the cigar box. (Durham Police)

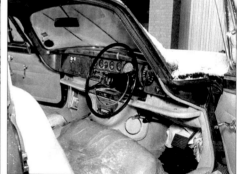

Above: Now it has disappeared, never to be seen again. Could this evidence belong to the killer?
(Durham Police)

Sibbet's glasses found by the police at the side of the A182 road along with cartridge cases, and fragments of collision debris.
(Durham Police)

e junction of the A182 with Pesspool Lane.
Inction House farm can be seen to the right
the main road, just before the junction.
le police discovered important forensic
vidence in the lane.
Vilson and Cowan, Sunderland.)

bove: Photograph 23. How the police envisage the two cars collided. (Durham Police)

Above: Photograph 21.Damage to Mark X
(Durham Police)

E-Type driving past camera at 30 mph under a sodium streetlamp,
illustrating the difficulties of seeing whether one or two people are inside.
(Media Arts)

Photograph 18. Damage to the rear of the E-Type (Durham Police)

Photograph 25. Mr Denton's reconstruction of the collision between the Mark X & E-Type. (Durham Police)

Disassembled engine of Mark X Jaguar. No pictures were taken of Number 5 cylinder showing the alleged 'bad' scoring (Durham Police)

Photograph 20. The E-Type and the Mark X side-by-side (Durham Police)

E-type Jaguar with rear light covers intact (above left) and broken (above right). (Media Arts)

Durham County Constabulary

STATEMENT FORM

Division _____ Station _____ Date _____

Name and Address _____ James GOLDEN,

5, Dene Avenue,

Easington Colliery.

33yrs.   Occupation _____ Blacksmith.

About 11.50 p.m. on Wednesday, 4th January, 1967, I was cycling towards Easington Village on my way home. When I was passing Burnips Farm, a Jaguar sports car, 'E' type, passed me going in the same direction as me, followed closely behind by an old type Jaguar car.

Both cars were travelling at about 60 m.p.h.

I did not see the occupants of either car.

(signed) J. Golden.

Statement taken at 11.50 p.m. 5.1.67. at South Hetton.
L. Hodgson. A/Sgt. 1161.

James Golden's three statements.
Above : Statement one.

Durham County Constabulary 45

STATEMENT FORM

Division _____ Station _____ 8.1.67.

Name and Address _____ James GOLDEN,

5, Dene Avenue,

Easington Colliery.

Age _____   Occupation _____ Miner.

Further to the statement I made on the 5th January, 1967, I might add that I left South Hetton Colliery at 11.45 p.m. to cycle to Easington Colliery on the 4th January, 1967.

When I had been riding my bicycle for about 10 minutes, two cars travelling from South Hetton passed me. I thought the two cars were both Jaguars. The first one was a 2 seater sports type and the second one was a large saloon, I was sure that was a Jaguar also. Both cars were being driven close together about 2 car lengths between them. I thought they were being driven at about 60 miles per hour. This was a fast road and the cars were going steady for the type of car on that particular road. I could not see what colour the cars were or how many people were in them.

Both cars passed me South Hetton side of Hutchinsons Farm, approximately 300 yards North of the farm entrance. They were travelling towards Easington Village and I paid no attention to them once they had passed me.

(signed) J. Golden.

Statement taken between 4.30 p.m. and 4.50 p.m. 8th January, 1967,
R. E. Richardson, D.C. 419. Regional Crime Squad.

Above : Statement two.

STATEMENT FORM

Division _____ Date _____ 10.1.67.

Name and Address _____ James GOLDEN,

5, Dene Avenue,

Easington Colliery.

Age 33 years.   Occupation _____ Blacksmith.

MR GOLDEN
should have
seen a
Police Patrol
or, the
occupants of
which did
n't see a
Mark 10 and
Type.
: BUS and
Moped.

About 11.45m on Wednesday, 4th January, 1967, I left South Hetton Colliery on my pedal cycle to ride home to Easington Colliery. I travelled through South Hetton under the Railway Bridge and continued along the main road. I continued on through the 30 m.p.h. slot. It was a dry clear night but the road is not lighted. I noticed nothing unusual on the road and in fact there was no other traffic on the road at that time. After I had been riding for about ten minutes and would be about 300 yards from the entrance to Hutchinson's Farm (near Pesspool Lane) the road was illuminated from my rear by a vehicle travelling in the same direction as me. I think that this vehicle was driving on headlights. It overtook me and I noticed that it was a 2 seater sports type Jaguar and when it had overtaken me another large saloon car also overtook me. From its shape I also think this car was a Jaguar and both vehicles were close together. The rear lights of the second car were lit. Both vehicles were being driven at 60 m.p.h. This is a fast speed but not so fast for the type of cars they were or the road they were on. I was unable to see how many occupants either car had.

After the cars had passed on I had to take my eyes off the cars to concentrate on the verge. They just continued on along the road towards Easington and at this point the road has a down gradient and has a left hand sweep and I am unable to say whether the cars continued to Easington or turned right into Pesspool Lane.

I saw no other vehicles on the road on my journey home and I heard no unusual noises. The weather was fine but when I arrived home about 12.10am it was just starting to snow.

(sgd.) J. Golden.

Statement taken at Peterlee Police Office between 4pm and 4.30pm on Tuesday, 10th January, 1967, by D. Critchlow. D/Inspector.

Left : Statement three.

View of right turn into Pesspool Lane off the A182 from 308 yards away.
A distance at which Superintend Kell swore on oath it was impossible to see the junction.

View of right turn into Pesspool Lane off the A182 from 528 yards away.

View of right turn into Pesspool Lane off the A182 from 628 yards away
Golden would have seen the lights of the E-Type and Mark X turning
into the Lane from each of these distances when cycling home.

Tom Fellows (left) with police artist Jan Szymczuk creating a portrait
of the man who visited him in Colin Dunn's garage in January 1967 (Photograph Media Arts)

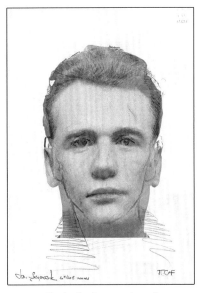

Portrait of a murderer?
How Tom Fellows remembers the man
who called himself Darren Reynolds,
as drawn by ex-Metropolitan Police
artist Jan Szymczuk overlayed onto
a photograph of Albert Donoghue
(Photograph Media Arts)

Top: Arthur Thompson's Mark X.
(Photographer Unknown)

Below: Christine Boyce, Reggie Kray and
Albert Donoghue (Photographer Unknown)

Dennis Stafford recently
(Brian Anderson)

Above: Michael Luvaglio receives an
award from HRH Prince Edward for his
charity work.
(Michael Luvaglio Family Album)

Left: South Hetton today, where Pesspool
Bridge has long since been demolished
along with the terrace on the right.
The Mark X has been overlayed to show
its position in 1967.
(Media Arts)

Michael Luvaglio recently during filming for the Footsteps In The Snow documentary.
(Media Arts)

cracked.'

On January 7, he again examined the Mark X at Peterlee and reported: 'The near side of the radiator grille and the associated horn grille had been pushed back; a number of the grille uprights were badly buckled and loose. The glasses of both off-side headlamps were broken and pieces of them were missing. There was a dent below the two off-side headlamps and one on the extreme near-side edge adjacent to the outer headlamp. The front number-plate showed a nearly complete circular impression which had severed the top corner of the left-side arm of the 'U' and made a deep impression in the top right-hand leg of the 'M'. To the left of this impression was a small impression which appears to be part of a similar impression.

Green paint was chipped off from the extreme near side adjacent to the headlamp, beside the radiator grille and nearside horn grille and between the two off-side headlamps. These areas were very slightly rusted. A number of bright red paint fragments were associated with the damage across the front of the vehicle. There were crushed bright red deposits near the top of the outer off-side member of the radiator grille and associated with damage to the extreme near side adjacent to the headlamp. There was a heavy smear of red paint present along the outer edge of the near-side rear bumper.'

The Prosecution Theory

Stanley Denton's version of events required the court to accept that between Pesspool Bridge, where the vehicles were seen by Mr Sanderson, and the collision and crime, the cars changed position twice. First the Mark X overtook the E-Type and then the sports car cut back in front of the saloon braking sharply and causing Sibbet's Mark X to run into its rear. All this supposedly took place in just over half a mile (1,092 yards), a distance that cars travelling at thirty mph, would have covered in about a minute.

From the witness box Mr Denton, a stocky man with thick-rimmed glasses and dark, brushed-back hair, explained his theory to Henry Scott: 'The vehicles could have arrived in this position, at the time of the accident, by the E-Type Jaguar cutting in front of the Mark X Jaguar and stopping at an angle to it. The force of impact may then have straightened up the E-Type Jaguar, the secondary impact having occurred as the Mark X tried to steer round the rear end of the E-Type Jaguar striking it at an angle. See Diagram 1 overleaf.

He had previously explained the various factors in his examination of the cars which had led to these conclusions: 'I am of the opinion that the region of the near-side radiator grille of the Mark X Jaguar collided with the rear near-side corner of the E-Type Jaguar, causing the majority of damage to both vehicles. A secondary impact of the extreme front near side of the Mark X Jaguar, in the region of the outer headlamp, with the paintwork at the top near side of the registration number-plate recess had also occurred.'

'Just looking at the photographs if we may,' requested Henry Scott, 'the

damage to which you are referring, the first impact, you visualise as being shown in photograph 23. Then another impact was when, if one looks at photograph 21, the damage to the extreme outer edge of the nearside headlamp was done?'
'Yes.'
'By contact with the same part of the near-side bumper of the E-Type?'
'No.'
'No?' repeated Mr Justice O'Connor in surprise.
'No. It was done by contact with the part of the bodywork above the letters in the registration number, causing that damage we can see in photograph 18.'
'Yes.'
'Yes, I beg your pardon. Causing the damage, we can see in photograph 18?'
'Yes.'

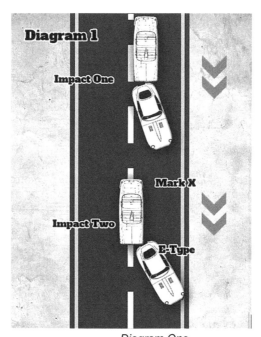

Diagram One

On January 10, in the yard of police station, Mr Denton had attempted to reconstruct the position of the cars at the moment of impact. Mr Scott asked him: 'By lining up the damaged area immediately above the 7 in the registration number [of the E-Type] with the red paint deposit on the outer off side of the radiator grille of the Mark X, did you find there was a good relative disposition?'

'Yes.'
'And also, the ends of the twin exhaust pipes on the E-Type with the damage to the front of the Mark X?'
'Yes.'
'Was the position of the red paint deposit on the extreme near side of the Mark X in good agreement with the damaged area above the registration number letters?'
'It was.'
'On consideration of the distance between the red paint deposits on the front of the Mark X, did that indicate they could not have been caused by a single impact with the E-Type?'
'Yes, Sir.'
'Just help us, Mr Denton,' asked Mr Justice O'Connor. 'About that last sentence. The distance between the red paint deposits on the front of the Mark X Jaguar indicated to you that they could not have been caused by a single impact'; Why?'
'Well, if you could look at photograph 21, I will point out the position where the red paint was deposited. There was one red paint deposit in this position on the off-side member and another red paint deposit at the same height in this position.'
'Yes.'
'And the distance between these two positions is much greater than the distance between the bumper over-riders of the E-Type Jaguar, and the only paint which was missing from the E-Type Jaguar, corresponding at the same height as these two positions on the Mark X Jaguar, were along the top of the Mark X Jaguar, were along the top of the registration number recess.'

A further impact link noted by Mr Denton was the damage to the registration plate of the Mark X Jaguar, which was apparently caused by impact with the twin exhaust pipes which protrude centrally from the E-Type.

In addition to the paint smears mentioned, Mr Denton had found pieces of glass, similar to the outer off-side headlamp of the Mark X, on the rear of the E-Type, balancing on top of the downward sloping bumper, and five tiny red plastic fragments from the E-Type's broken stop light on the Mark X bumper, amongst the smears of red paint.

In presenting Stanley Denton's theory about the collision, and the way in which he imagined the damage had been caused, we have assembled the pieces of evidence and quotations from his report - which he gave almost verbatim in court - in a way which we feel presents the prosecution case in the strongest and clearest light. In court the evidence was put forward in such a way that the jury could hardly have fail to grasp the point, essential to the prosecution's case, that a collision between the cars had taken place.

Shambles in Court

Key failings and improbabilities in Mr Denton's theory were not brought to the jury's attention and may well have been lost in the general complexity of the evidence. A confusion heightened by the prosecution's slip-shod presentation. When shown to the jury, for example, all the fragments of glass, paint and Perspex from the vehicles carried laboratory numbers entirely different to their re-assigned exhibit numbers. This led to the following, Alice in Wonderland like, exchanges.

Mr Scott: 'The only difficulty about it is that it bears from their [the jury's] point of view all the wrong numbers. I have had to renumber mine throughout.'

Mr Justice O'Connor: 'I am just setting to work to do it as we go along, but I think we can overcome that difficulty, but if you would like to consider it, Mr Lyons?'

Mr Lyons: 'Would your Lordship give me one moment?'

Mr Justice O'Connor: 'Yes, of course.'

Mr Scott: 'My Lord, perhaps I can carry on?'

Mr Lyons: 'My Lord, I have no objection.'

Mr Justice O'Connor: You see, it is a lot easier to follow if one has the thing in front of one. Have we got copies available now? In the groups of jurors, who-ever is responsible, would you have a pencil ready so we can mark in against the laboratory numbers the exhibit numbers. On the first page, 174 is 31, right at the top, and 68 is 20 and every time these two have occurred, half-way down the page, pencil in those exhibit numbers so that we can look at it in the evidence. ...202 is 49.'

Mr Denton: 'And 203 is 50.'

Mr Justice O'Connor: 'Yes, 20, 49 and 50.'

Mr Scott: 'In the samples of paint, 31 and 58 to 61, from the Mark X did you find a number of fragments?'

Mr Denton: 'May I interrupt? We don't seem to be getting the same exhibit numbers as you.'

Mr Scott: 'Let us be careful then. In the samples, 53, that is 174?'

Mr Denton: 'Yes.'

Mr Scott: 'And 209 which I make 56?'

Mr Denton: 'Yes.'

Mr Scott: 'And 210 which I make 57?'

Mr Denton: 'Yes.'

Mr Scott: 'And 212 to 214 which I make 58 to 61.'

Mr Denton: '59 to 61.'

Mr Scott: '59 to 61, is it?'

Mr Denton: 'Yes, that is correct.'

Mr Scott: 'And those had a number of fragments similar in layer and structure to exhibit 20 and 49?'

Mr Denton: 'Yes.'

Mr Scott: 'And those came from the E-Type in 31 and 59 to 61?'
Mr Denton: 'No, I don't think it is 207.'
Mr Scott: 'No. 54 to 58.' 207 is 54. 55, 56, and 57 and 58?'
Mr Denton: 'Yes, that is correct.'
Mr Scott: 'Those were all from the Mark X. In those did you discover a number of fragments similar in layer and structure to the paint in 51B?'
Mr Denton: '50.'
Mr Scott: '50B or 50A, I beg pardon?'
Mr Denton: '50A.'
Mr Justice O'Connor: 'I am just - 203A and B - Mr Denton is 50A and B.'
Mr Denton: 'Yes.'

A Clash of Experts

Since, for some reason, the defence called no expert motor witnesses to contest Mr Denton's conclusions, his evidence went unchallenged. Following the trial, the defence contacted George Bowman, a consultant motor engineer recommended by Professor Francis Camps. After examining the transcript, Mr Denton's report, the photographs and the vehicles themselves, he was able to point to nine aspects of the prosecution collision theory which their evidence had not explained. In his report he concluded: 'It is the considered opinion of Mr Denton that the collision between the Mark X and the E-Type Jaguar was the near-side radiator grille of the Mark X and the rear near-side corner of the E-Type. But all the photographs of the E-Type Jaguar, show no damage whatever to the near side of the E-Type. This point was confirmed on our visit to Peterlee police station on 14 March, when the only damage noted on the near side of the E-Type was a slight graze on the apex of the near-side rear bumper bar approximately twelve inches to the near side of the near-side over-rider.

We cannot reconcile the heavy damage to both off-side and near-side E-Type rear lamp lenses, when all the photographs of the E-Type show the reflector lenses undamaged and it is considered these would have suffered damage before the rear lamp plastic lenses. It is fair to assume, had the lenses shattered to the degree shown whilst attached to the motor car, the rear lamp casing would also have been damaged.

After our inspection at Peterlee police station we confirm the off-side rear lamp casing only is fractured at the junction between the rear lamp casing and the body panel. This fracture was caused by the distorted top flange of the off-side rear bumper blade forcing upwards, and it is our opinion, this distortion to the casing would have forced the lenses outwards after fracturing them round the screw-securing holes, which is usual on this type of lens. It is fair to assume, therefore, the off-side rear lamp lenses could have been broken by impact but not shattered to the degree shown in the photograph, and we cannot see how the near-side rear lamp lens was broken at all.

It is alleged by Mr Denton that the secondary impact, on the extreme near-side edge of the Mark X, was caused by striking the upper section of the E-Type rear number-plate. On studying the impact damage from the photograph and original bonnet at Peterlee police station there was no damage whatever to the adjacent Mark X headlamp rim, and from what we saw of this particular damage on the existing Mark X, the impact appears to have been square to the front of the Mark X, and had this been caused by evasive action, as suggested by Mr Denton, we would have envisaged the impact area to have been at an angle of approximately forty-five degrees.

We also consider, had this damage on the Mark X been caused by striking this particular area on the E-Type, we would have expected the damage on the E-Type to have been over a wider area, as it will be noted from photograph 25 the damage is square on to the front and consistent with striking a heavy, solid object.'

'It also occurs to us, had this particular impact occurred, we would have expected extensive damage to the E-Type twin exhausts as you will note from photograph 20, how much the near-side Mark X bumper protrudes beyond the vertical line of impact with the headlamp rim, and we would also have expected damage to the Mark X near-side flasher lens, on the extreme near-side comer immediately below the headlamp rim, which would have struck the lower section of the E-Type number-plate assembly.

We also cannot account for the red paint alleged to have been deposited on the near-side front of the Mark X bumper bar at this impact, as the bumper would have been well below any red paint areas on the E-Type and would most probably, in damaging the exhaust pipes, have practically demolished the reversing lamp.

Mr Denton alleges he found crushed dark green paint on the E-Type rear number-plate chrome surround, which was supposed to have been caused by contact with the Mark X chrome grille surround on which also had been found crushed paint. As both these alleged contact areas are chromium-plated steel, it is difficult to ascertain how these areas became contaminated with red and green paint.

Whether it was the near-side or off-side rear of the E-Type Jaguar coming into contact with the front of the Mark X Jaguar, it is difficult to believe how so much debris was found on the sloping bumper blade of the E-Type Jaguar, including the Mark X headlamp glass, when there was no debris whatever found on the front of the Mark X Jaguar. The design of the front end of the Mark X Jaguar, by virtue of the positioning of the front bumper blade and the bumper valance panel, lends itself quite readily for a large amount of debris to be retained.

It would be fair to assume quite a large amount of the off-side Mark X headlamp glass should have been found on the front of the Mark X, and had the rear lamp plastic lenses of the E-Type been fractured by contact with the Mark

X Jaguar we would have envisaged the major portion of these lenses should also have been found on the front of the Mark X bumper valance.

Again, if the two cars collided as alleged, with the E-Type bumper riding over the top of the Mark X bumper with all the damage, to the off-side E-Type rear bumper, it is fair to assume there would be damage to the off side of the Mark X bumper or over-rider that appeared to conform to the damage on the off-side underside of the E-Type (see photograph number 21) but during our inspection at Peterlee police station on 14 March 1968 the only abrasion that could be found on the Mark X over-rider was to the underside. We are still in doubt as to how it is alleged that red paint was found on both Mark X over-riders (off-side and near-side bumper sections) and the off-side and near-side of the centre section.

From what we see from the photographs, the paint marks on the off-side over-rider and off-side and near-side of the centre bumper blade could be attributed to at least three separate impacts with the E-Type, but we cannot explain the presence of the other paint marks.

In the view of Mr Denton all the evidence pointed to two collisions, occurring as shown in Diagram Two (overleaf). He was not, however, able to suggest the order in which these impacts occurred.

Impact One: Caused damage to the off-side front of the Mark X Jaguar in the vicinity of the off-side headlamp, and the off-side rear of the E-Type Jaguar. Photograph 24, above, shows the damage on the lower panel of the E-Type Jaguar, consistent with striking the off-side over-rider of the Mark X. The damage to the E-Type from this impact would be the off-side rear bumper, off-side over-rider, and the first dent shown in the lower panel on Photograph 24. The damage to the Mark X would have been both off-side headlamps, dents in the off-side front wing, dents in the off-side bonnet.

Impact Two: The near side of the Mark X radiator grille and again the off-side rear corner of the E-Type make contact. It appears the E-Type reversed into the front of the Mark X to account for the distortion of the Mark X radiator grille bars, chrome surround over to the near side, and the heavy crease in the near side of the Mark X bonnet square to the direction of impact, all shown in photograph 21.

If the Mark X had run into the E-Type, in a supposedly evasive action, the grille bars would most likely have been forced inwards. As Photograph 23 shows, there does not appear to be any distortion inwards whatever. The damage to the E-Type would be the offside rear bumper, together with the over rider, and probably the distortion of the off-side rear lamp casing and the long score mark on the off-side lower panel. The damage to the Mark X would be the near-side radiator grille surround, together with the grille bars and the heavy crease on the near side of the bonnet. Debris would have been red and green paint flakes and, most likely, rust flakes from the inside of the Mark X grille bars.

Impact Three: The offside and centre of the Mark X collided with the off side of the E-Type. Damage to the Mark X would have been exhaust marks on the front number plate while damage to the E-Type was most likely have been to the reversing lamp and exhaust pipes, Debris would have been top of the 'U' on the Mark X number-plate, reversing lamp glass on the E-Type and green and red paint.

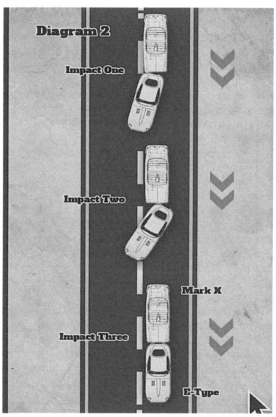

Diagram Two

Three Experts - Two Opinions

Let's start by reviewing the credentials of the 'experts, described by the judge as 'scientists,' who gave evidence for the prosecution. In addition to Stanley Denton, the court heard from DC McQueen, who did not appear in court but provided a sworn statement, and a Mr David Sunter, from Jaguar Cars. Both men were described in court as 'engineers' implying a high level of technical expertise. But, as Jaguar expert Mike Cassidy has pointed out to us: 'Mr Sunter was, in fact a motor mechanic rather than an experienced and qualified combustion engineer. DC McQueen, who carried out much of the mechanical investigation of the Mark X could also be more fairly described as a garage mechanic. It may be wondered whether these 'experts' on whom the court relied so heavily would have been able to carry out complex calculations on, for example, coefficients of expansion of dissimilar metals or the melting point of aluminium pistons as would a qualified engineer. Neither witness was challenged or examined on their competence to arrive at the opinions they reached.'

Stanley Denton described himself as a Licentiate of the Royal Institute of Chemistry (LRIC). The lowest entry-level for acceptance to the Institute, this suggests he was a chemist rather than a qualified crash or collision engineer. Yet he was being asked to make assessments of the complex damage to the bodywork of two vehicles.

'The single area where his chemistry qualifications might have helped,' suggests Mike Cassidy, 'would have been in the analysis of the paint samples. We can find no chemical analysis of the paint samples constituents and no spectroscopic or instrumental colour analysis having been performed. They seem to have simply been inspected under some kind of a microscope to examine the layers of paint. Finally, no attempt appears to be made to determine the number of red cars sold or the precise Jaguar red or whose paint had been used. Like the other experts, Mr Denton was never challenged on the relevance of his qualifications with regard to crash damage all the scientific or technical nature of the tests are carried out.'

These criticisms aside, George Bowman's analysis of the collision damage, seems so complete and valid it appears most unlikely that the collisions occurred in the way suggested by Mr Denton and the prosecution. The original court did not, of course, have the opportunity of considering Mr Bowman's evidence, but it was presented at the subsequent appeal to the High Court.

The curious juxta positioning of the cars, as proposed by Mr Denton, envisaged was contradicted by the photographic evidence, in particular and the prosecution theory as a whole. George Bowman's three-collisions theory explains the majority of the damage, with the exception of the small dent in the near-side front wing of the Mark X. For both experts the basic problem was relating the extensive damage to the whole of the front of the Mark X to the very limited damage to the rear of the E-Type, and the total destruction of the rear light and flasher lenses on both sides of the sports car when the surrounding areas were almost unmarked.

Both could be satisfactorily explained if a third vehicle and a deliberate attempt to link the cars were involved and, as we shall show, there are indications that this was indeed what happened.

Why so little attention was paid to the sole evidence against the accused, remains a mystery to us.

There is the testimony of Birdcage Club doorman, Matthew Dean, that a collision between the E-Type and another vehicle had taken place outside the club. Dennis Stafford and Michael Luvaglio say that the damage occurred sometime between when they left the car parked in Stowell Street, between 12.20 and 12.30, and when Dennis went out for cigarettes at about 2 o'clock.

The prosecution theory, as we have seen, was that both the murder and the collision took place at the same spot on the A182 opposite West Moor Farm.

It was along a stretch of this road, over a distance of some 136 feet, that various pieces of evidence were recovered, largely by DC Thomas Tipler. These included fragments of glass, red and amber Perspex, five cartridge cases, Sibbet's broken spectacles, and pieces of a mirror-type reflector. In Pesspool Lane more pieces of red and amber Perspex were found on the off-side verge and road and a piece of red Perspex, with metal foil attached, on the other side in the gutter one yard from the entrance to a field. There were also numerous discarded cigarette butts in the same location, but these were seemingly disregarded by the police because they did not fit into their theory. Although, in the days before genetic testing the information they might have provided was probably slight, a test on any saliva might well have revealed the blood group of the smoker. This is possible with 80 per cent of the population.

All the vehicle fragments were passed to Stanley Denton for examination. He matched many of them to one or other of the Jaguars. Perhaps the most satisfactory match, from the prosecution's point of view, was a piece of plastic from the number-plate of the Mark X. Mr Denton was asked by Henry Scott:

'Would you look, please, at Exhibit 23. That is the small piece of the 'U'?
'Yes, Sir.'
'Is that an exact physical fit with the remains of the 'U' on the number plate?'
'It is.'
'And I think you have photographed it fitted on to – in Exhibit 71 which I think the jury have already seen?'
'Yes.'
'Now, in the debris from Pesspool Lane, Exhibit 32, did that contain a large number of pieces of red and amber Perspex?'
'Yes.'
'Now this was from Pesspool Lane, have you fitted this together?'
'I have.'
'Did the majority of those pieces reassemble, Mr Denton?'
'Yes.'

Small fragments of Perspex from the rear light assemblies of the E-Type were found both on the A182 and in Pesspool Lane. Other important finds were pieces of Perspex stamped with the letters 'L' and 'D' which when reassembled provided the missing parts of the words 'LUCAS' and 'ENGLAND'. On the A182, police searchers found headlamp glass which matched the shattered off-side lights of the Mark X.

Clearly, then, there was convincing evidence to suggest the cars had collided along the A182. This is, by far and away, the strongest point in the prosecution case.

Did the Mark X Stop Because the Engine Seized?

In his opening speech, for the Crown, Mr Henry Scott had asserted the Mark X finally stopped there because the engine had been seizing: 'Had it not been for the Jaguar seizing up, heaven knows where this body would have ended up,' he went on. The sea, he added, was not far away and might have been a convenient place to dump the body. Although he also claimed, in his opening speech, the accused had 'raced back' to the Birdcage Club to establish an alibi.

The Mark X's engine had not, in fact, seized. According to the prosecution's own evidence, a single, small, hole in the radiator had caused it to overheat and stall. The court heard about this puncture from David Sunter, a motor engineer employed by Jaguar Cars. At the request of the Durham police he had gone to Peterlee police yard, on the morning of January 11, and attempted to fill the radiator with water. He said that he found one leak at the bottom of the radiator stack itself about four inches from the left-hand corner, in an area just behind the damaged struts of the grille. He explained to the court that this type of car is fitted with two torsion bars in a position approximately three quarters of an inch in front of the radiator on either side. Mr Castle-Miller asked him:

'Having regard to the damage which you saw to the front of the car, would that be consistent with the torsion bar being sprung back and so causing the damage?'
'Yes, Sir.'
'In your opinion is that what caused the leak?'
'It is, Sir.'

This seemed, initially, a clear and straightforward explanation. Under cross-examination, by Mr Dean, however Mr Sunter immediately contradicted himself.
'What is the diameter of the torsion bar roughly?' He was asked.
'Three eighths of an inch.'
'Because you see this hole in the front of the radiator is only about one eighth of an inch in diameter, isn't it?'
'I would have thought it slightly more than that.'
'Slightly more, as much as three eighths would you have thought?'
'No.'

'Could the hole have been caused by the end of a screwdriver, or some tool of that sort, used deliberately?'
'Oh, yes, yes, Sir.'
'Anything in the appearance of the hole to contradict that it is a possibility?'
'No.'

George Bowman too made a careful examination of the radiator and found not one but two holes. He reported: 'They were approximately of 3/16th of an inch apart and each hole was elongated vertically and measured approximately 5/32nd of an inch long. We did note, as the jagged metal had been forced inwards into the radiator core the direction of impact was approximately thirty degrees above the horizontal. The hole nearest to the near side appeared to have been punctured in a direction from the off side of the radiator and the second hole immediately from the front. It is very difficult to imagine how two clean holes, such as the ones noted, could have been caused by impact damage.'

According to Mr Sunter's measurements, the ends of the torsion bars were 12/32 of an inch wide, which would preclude them from having caused this damage, and there is no projection on the E-Type which could possibly be responsible. Accepting that there were leaks in the radiator, however caused, and that the water had drained away, what evidence is there than the saloon really had ground to a halt in such a very awkward place, under a street lamp, on a main road, in the middle of a village?

Mr Sunter told the court that when he examined the stripped-down 4.2 litre engine, he found that number five piston was quite badly scored, causing a knocking noise when the car was started up. Despite this, he was able to start the car in the police yard.

Mr Castle-Miller asked him how far the car might have travelled in that condition, assuming it was being driven at speed.
'A mile or so, but if it was driven quite lightly with regard to the fact that the engine had not got any water in then it may have gone several miles, maybe seven or eight miles altogether.'

It is a distance of roughly a mile from the alleged murder scene to the point in Pesspool Lane where the first stop was made. According to the witness James Golden, whose evidence we will discuss in the next chapter, the cars were travelling at some sixty mph. If one accepts the police account, they were then driven another five miles before the Mark X stalled just before the bridge. The A182 runs through open country and is derestricted. It was fundamental to the prosecution case that not a second could be wasted by the killers in order to get back to the centre of Newcastle just after midnight. Given that urgency, it seems reasonable to suppose that the cars travelled at speed. If so, by Mr Sunter's own evidence, it would have been impossible for the Mark X to have completed the journey to South Hetton. Indeed, if he is right, it would have stalled for good in Pesspool Lane. If he has underestimated the distance, or if the car was driven very gently, surely the engine must have been clearly protesting at such bad treatment. The temperature gauge would have been off the dial, there would have been a smell of overheated rubber and the pronounced knocking from number five cylinder which Mr Sunter noticed on 11 January. He told the court: '[the engine was] very noisy. There was a definite knock coming from the engine.'

Assuming the second alternative, let us put ourselves in the position of the driver of the Mark X. We are travelling along a lonely lane with a corpse propped up on the back seat, one window shattered by gunfire, with damage to the front bodywork and both off-side headlamps smashed, an engine which is quite plainly about to stall, in convoy with a sports car whose broken lights are glaring white. Under these circumstances we apparently decide to turn out from the shelter of the darkened lane and drive down a well-lit main road and through the centre of a mining village we know never sleeps.

The illogical decision of a panic-stricken man?

Perhaps. But the whole prosecution theory rests on the assumption that the accused acted with a cold and ruthless determination throughout. That they were the same men who could, after brutally slaying a close friend, spend two hours drinking and chatting in a night club without giving the slightest indication that anything untoward had happened?'

Again, assuming that the prosecution theory is correct, and that David Sunter was wrong when he concluded the engine had stalled, the only alternative is that it was deliberately left badly parked in a conspicuous location to attract attention. Left with an expectation that the body would rapidly be found. It is hard to see what the accused hoped to gain from such a dangerous manoeuvre. If Dennis Stafford and Michael Luvaglio are innocent, then other possibilities present themselves which we shall examine later.

An Anonymous Letter

On the 25 April 1973, at the time of Stafford and Luvaglio's appeal against their conviction, the Registrar of Criminal Appeals received the following letter. It read as follows: 'Sir, I have no idea whether this information is of any significance, but I feel that the Solicitors of DENNIS STAFFORD and MICHAEL LUVAGLIO, should be informed. On 7 January 1967, FRANK MORGAN ran the engine of the Mark 10 Jaguar without water which would give the impression of overheating this occurred in the Station Yard Peterlee. I am confident that MAC noticed the difference of Engine condition on later inspection of the vehicle in question.With a family to consider it obvious that I can't put my name to this letter, but I swear it is the truth, and a few enquiries will reveal that this is common knowledge.' It was signed 'FOR JUSTICE'.

This suggested that the Mark X engine's seizure may well have been the result not of collision, but a deliberate act to incriminate the accused.

As every police officer, lawyer and investigative journalist knows, whenever there is a major criminal case all sorts of people emerge from the woodwork. They offer a wide range of frequently bizarre, unlikely or completely impossible theories. Sometimes their letters reveal indicate their lack veracity by the way they are written, or the colour of the ink used. Whilst the use of capitals in this anonymous letter raises some alarm bells in our minds, the content seems plausible. Whether or not you feel it adds anything to the case or should be trusted is a matter for you decide when reaching your verdict.

Evidence That Never Was

We have now dealt with nearly all the material evidence relating to the condition of the cars. One further matter, which occupied a considerable amount of the court's time, illustrate the point that a prosecution case based largely on conjecture can explain evidence in a way that, while completely logical, is also incorrect. The particular item of evidence in question is a dent in the top near side of the Mark X radiator grille. The explanation Stanley Denton provided is, perhaps, a further illustration of his lack of engineering knowledge. When cross-examined by Mr Raymond Dean, Denton initially felt unable to say how it might have occurred: 'I could not find any parts that would cause that damage,' he admitted when first questioned. A few moments later, during cross-examined by Mr Lyons, he suddenly came forward with a new theory:

'It is not inconceivable that the damage was caused by the E-Type over-rider riding up at the time of the accident, but I cannot find anything to connect that particular mark with the E-Type.'

'What you said before was that you could not find that any part of the E-Type could have caused that dent.'

'Well, I have just been thinking it over.'

'You are changing your mind, are you?'

'I think it is a possibility.'

'Just look at photograph 20, please, where the two cars are side by side.'

'Yes.'

'Was the ground flat there?'

'It slopes slightly.'

'There is no doubt is there that the bumper bars at the back of the E-Type are very much lower in height than the top of the radiator grille of the Mark X?'

'They are lower, yes.'

'Well, the projecting part of the E-Type is very much lower, is it not, than the dent on the top of the Mark X radiator?'

'It is lower, but I think that the perspective of the photographs tends to make it look lower than it really is.'

It is difficult to see how Mr Denton was able to reconcile this explanation with his previous evidence, when he said that the rear of the E-Type had ridden up over the Mark X bumper to force in the struts at the bottom of the radiator. The prosecution however not only accepted it but recalled Mr Sunter

specifically to confirm the supposition. Mr Henry Scott asked him:
'If the brakes are put on suddenly on a Mark X, what would be the effect on the E-Type?'
'The back end would come up, would rise.'
'Roughly, how much?'
'Five inches maybe.'
'Would the rising of the leading car and the sinking of the second car bring the over-rider into contact with the dent on the top of that car?'
At this point Mr Justice O'Connor enquired: 'Which photograph are you looking at?'
'Number 23, My Lord.'
'Well, you cannot very easily see the dent in that.'
'No, it is not very easy, My Lord. One can see the dent. One can see where it is.'
'I know where the dent is,' the judge retorted sharply. Then added: 'Photograph 21 was the one we were talking about'.
'Can you judge from that whether the rising of one and the falling of the other would bring those two into contact?'
'Yes,' the judge replied satisfied. 'I think it would.'

The cars brake, the rear of the E-Type rises up while the front of the Mark X drops down and a radiator is dented. Perhaps, despite the conflicting positions of the damage, the jury accepted this explanation as logical. Certainly, the judge, the lawyers and the prosecution's experts were convinced.

It was unfortunate that, before indulging in these mental gymnastics, they had not looked more carefully at the photographs of the Mark X taken by the police cameraman at 5.45 am on 5 January. These show quite clearly that there was no such dent in the grille surround at this time. It was in fact caused by a towing hook during the saloon's long, slow driverless journey to Peterlee. But not until all the defence evidence had been concluded did this simple truth emerge.

Police Work – Then and Now

In the Sixties, the police acted entirely on 'information received'. This would normally be a paid informant, and often somebody with a powerful motive to provide information which may have been wholly inaccurate. One drug dealer might provide information about another to put him out of business or as an act of revenge or, of course, to divert police away from the true culprit.

Before the introduction of tape-recorded interviews in the 1980s, the police would regularly invent verbal admissions. Sometimes it was the only evidence against a defendant, and many were convicted purely on the basis of disputed confessions. The practice became notorious as 'verballing' and the same phrases, starting with 'It's a fair cop' and graduating to the slightly more sophisticated 'What can I say?' or 'You know everything already...' were rehearsed hundreds of times in criminal courts.

'Verballing' meant that the defendant had to attack the police through his counsel. That in turn meant that when the defendant gave evidence, the prosecutor was allowed to cross-examine him on his previous convictions. Juries therefore learned that a person accused of armed robbery already had convictions for similar offences, so it was much more likely that he was guilty of the current charge, particularly as the police obviously had information leading to his arrest which, presumably, they couldn't use.

There were, of course, numerous allegations that police planted evidence like drugs or firearms. Then, without DNA, there was no significant risk in doing so. This is not to say that all police officer were dishonest: far from it; but they were under pressure to achieve results and if, for example, they received information from several sources to the effect that a person was responsible for a particular robbery, they might find themselves unable to do anything if the person they arrested simply denied it and none of the informants was prepared to give evidence or even able to do so because he lacked knowledge of the offence himself.

So it was that manipulating evidence or, more bluntly, fitting people up became relatively commonplace. Police officers who engaged in this activity no doubt believed that they were acting in a 'noble cause' and quite probably they achieved justice of a kind in most instances.

Police investigations have changed dramatically during the last fifty years. The investigative tools are far more powerful. Modern police can rely on:
- CCTV to track people's movements in almost any built-up area.
- Automatic number plate recognition (ANPR) enables them to track motor vehicles on motorways and main roads.
- Anyone carrying a mobile phone can be tracked live. All mobile phone companies keep the full call data records for a minimum of one year. The police can therefore trace their location throughout that period as long as the person concerned is carrying a phone. Unknown to many criminals, this applies even if the phone has been switched off.
- Mobile phones usually yield a mass of further information about people's contacts, messages, interests and motives. Deleted material can nearly always be recovered. Many defendants have been convicted purely on the basis of their mobile phone traffic, for example receiving calls from accomplices at critical times, suggesting that even if they are not directly involved in, say, a drug transaction, they are supervising or being kept informed of developments.
- DNA has revolutionised forensic science. The tiniest trace of, for example, saliva at the scene of a crime or on a gun or stolen goods has often led to a conviction with little supporting evidence. The size of such samples is usually microscopic and invisible. So sensitive are the techniques now that courts have to be cautious about relying on them, as, for example, if A shakes hands with B and B shakes hands with C, it is quite likely that A's

DNA will be on C's hands although they have never even met. The same issue arises with samples recovered from objects where tertiary transfer cannot be excluded.

- The courts now allow 'bad character evidence'. This is a complex subject, but there are now numerous opportunities for the Prosecution to introduce a person's previous convictions as long as the prosecutor is able to persuade the judge that those convictions or other bad conduct is relevant to an issue in the case.

- Any defendant putting forward an alibi defence now needs to be extremely cautious because the police will be able to check up not only on his/her movements but those of the alibi witnesses and, of course, all their communications and locations.

When Sibbet was murdered the police lacked any of the tools now available, and so had little choice but to create their own! In the 1960s, a famous associate of the Krays was accused of armed robbery. His wife was seeing a Harley Street gynaecologist at the time. He prevailed on the doctor to invent an appointment for his wife on the day of the robbery and to confirm that the robber had attended with her that day. The evidence was created by writing her name in a diary.

If he were to create such an alibi now, it would be discredited instantly. The appointment would be recorded in a computer. It would be possible to determine exactly when and probably by whom that entry had been made. The appointment would almost certainly have been made by phone and the call data records would establish whether any such a call had been made, quite apart from the location of the caller and the person receiving the call if on a mobile. It is highly likely that the journey to the gynaecologist would have been recorded on numerous CCTV cameras if it took place. Wherever we go and whatever we do, we now leave a digital trail. Even a bus pass can land you in jail, as the Hatton Garden robbers discovered.

Against this background we suggest that the fabrication or manipulation of the collision evidence was by no means an unlikely scenario in the 1960's. It is surely very odd that when PC McQueen started the Mark 10 on 6th January 1967, he recorded the fact that it was in good mechanical order. Four days later when the Mark 10 was started, it was noted that the radiator was punctured and leaking badly. The engine was also knocking. We also know that an anonymous informant, who must have been a police officer because he even knew the names of the officers involved, reported to the Defence that the Mark 10 had been run in the police yard. It is suggested that there would have been little point in simply running the car: it is more likely that the vehicle was being driven or at least moved. Given that it was supposed to be preserved as an essential crime scene, why drive it around? The only obvious answer is so that it could be placed in position with the E-Type so as to stage a collision. This might account for the curious evidence in relation to the apparent number of collisions and how the radiator got damaged.

We have no evidence that the collision damage was fabricated in this way. It is inherently unlikely that we would. There have been numerous well-reported cases of endemic police corruption, for example the West Midlands Serious Crime Squad; the Clubs Office in the West End of London, the Flying Squad at Scotland Yard; the Pick-pocketing Squad, who became known as the Pony Trekkers. They would watch out for anyone with a criminal conviction, especially for pick-pocketing, and claim to have witnessed such an offence unless the person happened to have a pony (£25) they could give them to go away. Perhaps the most notable feature of this corruption is that it was almost never exposed by a police officer. Very strong social ties unite the police. It is extremely rare for an officer to break ranks.

In the late 1970s Operation Countryman led to the forced resignation of over 250 police officers. Again, it was not initiated by a police officer, but by a 'Supergrass'. In fact, senior police officers obstructed the investigation relentlessly. Its findings were too embarrassing to publish.

Chapter Eleven: The Cyclist Who Heard Nothing in the Night

*'I say you cannot see the junction of Pesspool Lane and the A.182 road
from three hundred yards north-west of that junction which is the South
Hetton side.' Superintendent Ronald Kell*

As Nora Burnip left the court, after giving her evidence about hearing what had sounded like gunshots, on the night of January 5th, James Golden, a powerfully built, fair-haired, young 33-year-old stepped into the witness box. After giving his name, and address in Easington Colliery, he told the court how he finished work at South Hetton colliery at 11.15 pm, showered, changed and set off for home on his bicycle. This, he initially said, was at 11.40 pm.

In the three statements he gave to the police, from which we quote below, at no time did he mention leaving the colliery as early as 11.40. In the first he gave the time as 11.50, but in the next two said it was 11.45. This matters because, as we will explain, the earlier to left work the more easily what happened next matches the police version of event. At the trial, Raymond Scott asked him:

'As you cycled along do you remember something happening?'

'Just the two cars passing me, Sir.'

'That is what I want to ask you about. What sort of cars were they?'

'Two Jaguars, Sir. One was a sports, E-Type, and the other one was a saloon.'

'Which order were they in?'

'The sports car was in front.'

'At what speed were they going then?'

'Probably about sixty mph.'

'Is that the sort of road where that sort of speed would excite your attention?'

'No, not really.'

'Apart from seeing them going past you did you pay them any other attention?'

'Well, what drew my notice to them was that they were travelling that close together.'

'But once they got past you did you watch what happened to them?'

a. No, no Sir.

'Now, I would like to know, if I can, about where it was they went past you. I don't know whether the map will help you greatly. Perhaps you might look at some of the aerial photographs?'

'See if we can get it from the plan first of all, Mr Scott,' the judge instructed.

'Yes, My Lord. Let us try it from the plan. On your route home did you go under that bridge?'

'Yes, Sir.'

'Did you get beyond that?'

'Yes, Sir.'

'Then there is a turning off called West Lane? Did you get beyond that?'

'Yes, Sir.'

'And then the next building reached, of any importance, is West Moor House, which is a farm on your right?'

'Yes, Sir.'

'Did you get past that?'

'Yes, Sir.'

'And then the next place is Junction House and just beyond it is Pesspool Lane?'

'Yes, Sir.'

'Did you reach Junction House?'

'No, Sir.'

'How far short of Junction House were you?'

'About three hundred yards I should think.'

'What time was it, or would it be, that they passed you? How long had it taken you to cycle that far?'

'Well, probably be about ten to twelve. It takes me about ten minutes to cycle to that spot from the colliery.'

'What time did you get home?'

'It was about five past twelve.'

After a few more questions about the weather conditions Mr Scott asked him finally:

'Had you heard anything before the cars overtook you?'

'No, Sir.'

This point was immediately seized upon by Mr Dean, who rose and enquired:

'No sound of shots, or anything resembling the sound of shots?'

'No. Sir.'

'All was quiet?'

'Yes, Sir.'

'And you cycled steadily along the road from the colliery on your way home, the whole stretch of that road from Pesspool Bridge down to where you were when the cars passed you?'

'Yes, Sir.'

Mr Lyons followed the same line as his colleague when he took up the cross-examination:

'During that time did you overtake any stationary motor car?'

'No, Sir.'

'And you heard nothing at all?'

'No, Sir.'

'Did you ever hear any squeal of brakes or anything like that?'

'No, Sir.'

'During that time did you overtake any stationary motor car?'

'No, Sir.'

'And you heard nothing at all?'

'No, Sir.

Perhaps, at first reading, it seems to you - as it must have done to the jury - only slightly odd that James Golden failed to hear the shots, the shattering of window glass as the rear off-side window was blown out and the noise of a collision at speed between two heavy vehicles. Odd but of no great significance. The jury never heard any evidence relating to Golden's speed or the distances he had to cover on his way home, which was a serious omission. His evidence, if it is to be believed, and there is absolutely no reason to doubt this prosecution witness, was the most vitally significant in the whole trial. There is no way it can be reconciled to the prosecution theory once the full implications have been understood.

What Golden's Evidence Really Tells Us
James Golden stated he was about three hundred yards short of Junction House when he was overtaken by the Jaguars. So where was he, on the A182, while the murder was taking place? The question can be answered by considering just two variables. The first is his cycling speed, the second the total time taken by the murderers, starting from the moment the cars collided and ending when they overtook Golden. By calculating the number of yards Golden would travel at different speeds during different time periods, one can discover approximately where he was on at the time when, if the police are to be believed, the murder was being committed.

Let us first consider Golden's speed. This will allow us to arrive at a reasonable upper and lower limit for whereabouts on the A182 he was likely to have been when, according to the police, Sibbet was shot dead. On oath he said that he cycled the whole distance, he didn't get off to push his bike at any time. Golden, a fit young man hurrying home from work on a bitterly cold night is unlikely to have paused to catch his breath or take in the view. It seems reasonable to conclude he peddled as hard as he could to complete the four-mile ride between the colliery and his house.

After the trial a private detective was employed by the defence to follow him home and, using a stopwatch, made an accurate record of his times between important fixed points. These were as follows:
Time taken to reach West Moor Farm (alleged scene of crime) 4 min 18 sec.
Time taken to reach Pesspool Lane 7 min 37 sec.
Mr Norman Bennett, a surveyor for the defence, took precise measurements of the distances over which Golden was timed:
South Hetton Colliery to West Moor Farm, 1,666 yards.
West Moor Farm to Golden was overtaken by the two cars, 1,208 yards.

From these two sets of figures we can easily calculate Golden's average speed from the colliery to West Moor Farm. He covered the distance of 1,666 yards in four minutes eighteen seconds which gives him an average speed of 19.3 feet per second, or approximately 13 m.p.h.

The second timed section of his journey, from the farm to Pesspool

Lane, took him three minutes nineteen seconds. Since a large part of this is downhill, we would expect a higher average speed, but to calculate it we have to include the distance from the point 300 yards short of Junction House (where the surveyor finished his measurement) to Pesspool Lane. An accurate large-scale plan of the area gives a distance of about 104 yards from Pesspool Lane to Junction House. Golden, therefore, travelled a total of 1,208 yards + 300 yards + 104 yards= 1,612 yards in three minutes 19 seconds, or at an average speed of 16.5 mph.

When the detective took his timings, the road was shrouded by dense fog. On the night of the murder it was cold but clear with no snow on the road. It seems likely, therefore, the average speed of 14.75 mph, which we arrive at on the basis of the above calculations, is a conservative estimate.

The police allowed a time of four minutes from the moment of collision to the moment of get-away. To this we must add the time taken for the murderers to move off, accelerate to approximately sixty mph and overtake Golden 1,208 yards away. We think it reasonable to allow one minute for this, which gives the cars an average speed from standstill of about forty-one mph. It would seem most unlikely that the whole murder operation could have occurred in less than two minutes. Sibbet was, as we have said, a large, heavy, man. It would have been quite a struggle for two slightly built men like Stafford and Luvaglio to do what the police alleged they had done. That is, drag him around the car, in a 'sort of shunting motion', heave him onto the grass verge and then pull and push him into the rear compartment of the Mark X. This, we must emphasise, is what the prosecution claim happened and not what we believe or accept happened.

Again, working within the tight limits of the timetable, which the prosecution had to devise in order to explain how Stafford and Luvaglio could have arrived at the Birdcage no later than twelve thirty, five minutes would seem to be a reasonable upper time limit.

In the diagram overleaf, we have calculated Golden's position on the road for a speed of between 12 and 16 mph, allowing between three and six minutes for the collision, shooting, heaving a corpse into the Mark X and driving away. The critical importance of all this can be seen from Diagram Four below. Here we have projected Golden's position back down the A182 for four possible time-speed combinations.

Diagram Three – Aerial photograph of A182 and land around West Moor Farm showing the position of James Golden at various cycling speeds

First Cycle Icon from right: Golden's position on A 182 if cycling at 12 mph and the entire killing occurred two minutes. That is in half the police estimate. Golden would have been 128 yards away from the cars when the murder occurred. While, under these circumstances he might not have seen anything he would surely have heard two cars colliding at speed and gunshots fired on the still January night.

Second Cycle Icon: Golden's location if he was cycling at 14 mph, close to his average as measured by the private detective. As noted above, the detective recorded this speed under foggy conditions rather than the clear night of the murder. The time to commit the murder, dispose of the body and speed off now increases to three minutes. Golden would have been only a few yards short of the alleged scene when the collision occurred and must have cycled past as Sibbet was being shot dead.

Cycle Icons Three and Four: Golden's position along the road if cycling at either 14 mph, and allowing 5 minutes for the murder, or 16 mph with 4 minutes for the murder.

Both make clear something the other cycle speed and murder time combinations reveal. If the prosecution theory is correct, Golden must have cycled past the scene, and swung out to overtake the impacted cars at the very moment whilst the murderer was being committed. The fact he did not do so strongly suggests this crucial aspect of the police case must be wrong. But there are other problems with this witness, as the police quickly realised and took steps to overcome.

The Three Statements of James Golden

On 5 January at 11:50 pm, eighteen hours after the discovery of the body, Golden gave a statement to police in South Hetton. He told them that on the 4 January at 11:50pm he had been overtaken by an E-Type and an old Jaguar car as he was cycling past West Moor Farm. At this point in their inquiry the police had not yet established either the time or the scene of the murder.

Once Chief Superintendent Kell had charged Dennis and Michael, it became critically important to show the murder had occurred within a very short time frame. On the afternoon of January 8, he was invited to make a second attempt. In this longer version of events, he shifted the time he left the colliery from 11.50 to 11.45. After cycling for ten minutes, he says he was overtaken by a two-seater sports type and a large saloon. They were about two car lengths apart and travelling, at around 60 mph, towards Easington Village. He was unable to say what colour they were or how many people were in them.

Still not entirely satisfied, Kell asked Golden for a third statement. This he made on the afternoon of January 10. His first statement had been taken by an acting sergeant and the second by a Detective Constable.

For the third a Detective Inspector asked the questions. While Golden did not change his revised departure time from the colliery, he elaborated on his description of the two vehicles:

'After I had been riding for about 10 minutes and would be about 300 yards from the entrance to Hutchinson's farm near Pesspool Lane, the road was illuminated from my rear by a vehicle travelling in the same direction as me. I think that this vehicle was driving on headlights. It overtook me and I noticed that it was a two-seater sports type Jaguar and when it had overtaken me another large saloon car also overtook me. From its shape I also think this car was a Jaguar and both vehicles were close together. The rear lights of the second car were lit. Both vehicles were being driven at about 60 mph. This is a fast speed but not so fast for the type of cars they were or the road they were on. I was unable to see how many occupants either car had. After they had passed on, I had to take my eyes off the cars to concentrate on the verge. They just continued along the road towards Easington and at this point the road has a down gradient and has a left hand sweep and I was unable to say whether the cars continued to Easington or turn right into Pesspool Lane I saw no other vehicles on the road on my journey home and I heard no unusual sounds. The weather was fine but when I arrived home about 12.10 it was just starting to snow.'

The third statement did not mention of the two previous ones, nor were they mentioned by the prosecution. This left the jury the impression that had only one had been made. The defence were never told of these earlier statements or that he had changed his departure time from the colliery, from 11.50 to 11.45, between the first and second. He had also sifted his location further along the A182. Rather than positioning himself opposite Burnip's Farm, as in his first statement, he now claimed to have been closer to Hutchinson's Farm which is, itself, closer to the junction between the A182 and Pesspool Lane.

Why was the existence of three, slightly differing, statements never revealed to the defence? Nothing especially sinister need necessarily be read into this. Unlike today, when the prosecution has a legal obligation to disclose not only material relied on in court, but all the evidence gathered, at the time of the trial things were very different. Whether or not a document as given to the defence was entirely a matter for the prosecution. Any crumbs they did throw the defences way was a matter or professional courtesy between barristers rather than a necessity. In this case they chose not to reveal the three statements, nor a mass of other evidence which ran contrary to their case.

One further curious point. It would have been an easy matter to check the precise time James Golden left the colliery that night, by reference to his timecard. Every employee at the mine was required to clock on and off shift, so a permanent and accurate departure time could have been obtained and presented in court. We know, as stated earlier, the police did check the time-cards of a number of miners. These presumably included Golden. Rather than offer this firm evidence they preferred to rely on his recollection of the time. One might speculate this was because 'recollections' are more amenable to manipulation than the official record. It is also strange that the defence did not seek to test his statement against a timecard, given its critical importance to their case.

There are other aspects of Golden's evidence which should be considered. At the committal proceedings he told magistrates he was able to identify the leading vehicle as an E-Type Jaguar and the second as a Jaguar saloon. If the sports car had just been involved in the collision, then both rear lights would have been glaring white and Golden would surely have noticed this (see photos in the photographic section).

But he did not. Nor, despite an immensely thorough investigation and wide publicity, did anybody come forward to say they had seen a damaged Jaguar travelling at high speed through several villages and finally through the centre of Newcastle, as the police claimed must have happened.

The Junction with Pesspool Lane
Debris had been found in Pesspool Lane, it was the prosecution's case that after the murder the two vehicles had turned right into this small and winding country road, about three hundred yards in front of Golden. Yet when he gave his evidence, on February 15, 1967, he told the Peterlee magistrates: 'I did not see where they went after they passed me.'

The question was could he had seen them?

Two days after he had given evidence, Superintendent Kell told the court: 'An inquiry was set in train last night into the visibility on the A 182 road. I inspected it this morning. I say you cannot see the junction of Pesspool Lane and the A182 road from three hundred yards north-west of that junction which is the South Hetton side. The junction becomes clear from about a hundred yards. The junction could be seen from a distance of four hundred yards because I was then on the brow of a hill looking down on it.'

The defence made their own investigations and, at the trial, called surveyor Mr Norman Bennett who had made a series of measurements on the A182. Mr Taylor asked him:

'Would you look at the two photographs which are Exhibit 88. Were you present when these photographs were taken?'

'I was.'

'And were they taken from places which you had marked?'

'They were.'

'The photograph marked 3, what distance from Pesspool Lane was that taken?'

'This was taken at a point which I showed on my plan as Point C.'

'And what distance was that from Pesspool Lane?'

'Point C was fourteen chains.'

'Can you translate that into yards?'

'At twenty-two it will be 308.'

'308 yards?'

'308. Twenty-two yards to the chain.'

'And the other photograph number 4, was that taken from your point E?'

'This was taken from point E, which was twenty-four chains, 528 yards.'

'And from these two points, and your other points, that you indicate at various distances, and which I will ask you about in a moment, was it possible at these points you marked to see the junction with Pesspool Lane?'

'Yes, it was clearly possible.'

'So, we know it is possible to see it from 308 and 528 yards. From your other point did you check the distance?'

'To the point marked G it was thirty-one chains, 682 yards.'

'And between points C and E which were 308 yards and 528 yards, was there another point D?'

'There was a point D which was nineteen chains, 418 yards.'

'Was it visible from there too?'

'It was quite visible from there.'

According to his unchallenged evidence, the junction could be seen continuously between a distance of 308 yards and 682 yards, and also continuously up to 308 yards. Nor was this an isolated case. After the trial Mr Bennett made further measurements as he attempted to mark out the extent of the debris at the alleged scene of the crime.

In his report of December 4, 1967, he pointed out a further grave error in the police evidence. 'All measurements are taken from the field entrance to a temporary point (e.g. cartridge case) and then a check measurement is given between two fixed points - the field entrance and a tree - and accordingly I find this distance is some 256 feet, and not 136 feet 5 inches as shown by the plan supplied by the police. As a chartered surveyor it would be difficult for me to accept any of the other measurements if such a large discrepancy existed in the only one it was possible to check.'

Was a Silencer Used?

From the police point of view the second uncomfortable fact which emerges, even from this helpfully modified statement, was Golden's failure to hear the gun shots that had roused Nora Burnip from her bed. Failed to hear them despite the fact that, if the prosecution case was correct, he must have been almost on alongside the gunman when he pulled the trigger.

How could the evidence of the cyclist who heard nothing in the night, be explained? The prosecution did their best. George Price the ballistics expert thought that a 7.65 mm automatic pistol had been used and this evidence was unchallenged. Can a silencer be fitted to this type of weapon? The jury seemed to have believed it was possible, the police ballistics expert did nothing to challenge the assumption and the defence produced no evidence to refute it.

Shortly after the trial we sought the opinion of Mr L. J. Pearce, managing director of Churchill (Gunmakers) Ltd of London. He told us: 'I have never seen a silencer fitted to an automatic pistol of this type. From inquiries I have made, no such silencer has ever been produced.'

As we have shown, on several key aspects of the case, Superintendent Kell and his senior officers were either mistaken, misinformed or mendacious. If the former, we can only say that such blatant inaccuracies are not to be expected from a team of detectives led by Chief Superintendent. If the latter it sharpens our suspicions that, throughout the case, the police sought to mould the evidence to match a theory they had reached within hours of the body being found. Dennis Stafford was responsible, and they would make sure he did not escape justice. Whatever it took.

Chapter Twelve: The Summing Up

*'Today is the exact anniversary of the uttering of that famous cry which
has rung down through the ages when Julius Caesar lay dying, "And you Brutus,"
whose dagger was in his heart. His friend.'*
Mr Justice O'Connor summing up the evidence.

Early in the afternoon of Tuesday, March 14, Mr Justice O'Connor turned to face the jury and began his summing-up of a trial which had lasted five and a half days and heard evidence from sixty-four witnesses. During the lunch adjournment, the general feeling amongst lawyers, court officials and members of the public who had heard all the evidence, was that an acquittal seemed virtually certain. In near-by pubs, where the case was the chief topic of conversation, betting heavily favoured a Not Guilty verdict. But by the time the jury retired, at 2.17 the following afternoon, both public opinion - and the odds - had completely reversed. Rightly or wrongly, this change of mood can only have been occasioned by the judge's summing-up. Here was a case of considerable complexity, where there was no motive and no direct evidence to implicate either accused.

We criticise this summing-up firstly on the grounds that Mr Justice O'Connor sought to challenge evidence only when it was in the interests of the prosecution to do so, and secondly that he used language and metaphors of a highly emotive kind to express the simplest statements. Earlier we debated what influence the two men's involvement in an entertainments and gambling organisation and their way of life in general might have had on a Newcastle jury in 1967. Mr Justice O'Connor left little doubt of his own views when he said: 'It may be a way of life which is repellent to some or all of you, but you are not trying Luvaglio and Stafford for living what some of you may consider a very immoral life. They are not being tried because they are unfaithful to their wives or mistresses.'

Michael Luvaglio was unmarried, and the term 'mistress' carried, entirely undeservedly, prejudicial overtones. Again, when talking about Social Club Services, he said the company was 'engaged in activities which, as I have said, you may think were not very desirable in a community, but please put it from your mind'.

Before reviewing his summing up in detail, let's take a look at the background of the judge involved.

The Making of Judge O'Connor

Patrick McCarthy O'Connor was, to use an American term, a 'Cradle Catholic' steeped in that religion's moral beliefs from his earliest years. He was born in India, on December 28, 1914, the son of an Irish Catholic missionary doctor. Home educated to the age of eleven, he was then sent as a boarder to England's foremost Catholic school, Downside Abbey, in South West England.

From Downside he studied law at Merton College, Oxford before joining the Inner Temple at the start of the Second World War.

Poor health prevented him from serving in the forces and he spent the war on fire watching duties whilst building up a lucrative libel practice. In 1966, he was appointed a High Court Judge, attached to the Queen's Bench Division. Less than six months later he presided over the trial of Stafford and Luvaglio. Although an able civil lawyer, he was for years legal officer to the Post Office, O'Connor had little or no experience of conducting a criminal trial. Certainly, he had no experience or understanding of, an even less sympathy with, the occupations and lifestyles of the accused.

The bias and prejudice against those he considered sinful, and the strong pro-prosecution bias he displayed throughout in the trial, found an eerie echo, some twenty years later. In 1988, he was one of the judges hearing in the second appeal by a group of prisoners known as the Birmingham Six.

On the 21 November 1974, explosive devices had been placed in two Birmingham pubs the Mulberry Bush and the Tavern in the Town. Twenty people were killed and almost two hundred injured. The following year six Irishmen were sentenced to life imprisonment on, as the court admitted almost twenty years later, the basis of trumped up evidence and police falsehoods. At the men's second appeal most of those following the case were certain, as in the case of Stafford and Luvaglio, the convictions would be quashed. Mr Justice O'Connor and Lord Justice Lane disagreed. For his part, O'Connor decided the defendants had 'not only lied but had jointly concerted their lies'. He ridiculed the idea that the schedule of police interviews was a blueprint for perjury. 'With no disrespect to Mr Reade [who headed the investigation],' 1 O'Connor remarked: 'Whatever else might be said about him, he was clearly not a person who was capable of organising such a huge and complicated conspiracy.' If the document had been the foundation for a false case, it was, he added, a 'remarkably inefficient one'.

For four hours, the two judges took it in turns to go through the evidence item by item, giving their reasons for rejecting every one of the defence arguments. As a result of their opposition, six innocent men spent a further three years behind bars. Only after fresh evidence of police dishonesty was uncovered in 1991, by Granada's World in Action, were the convictions were overturned and the 'Birmingham Six' walked from the court as free men. The extent of Mr Justice O'Connor's desire to encourage the jury to view the prosecution's evidence in the strongest possible light, is well illustrated by his discussion of the blood on the Mark X's transmission tunnel. After pointing out that it implicated neither accused, he asked: 'Was there another person in the murdering gang?'

1 In 1993 ex-Detective Superintendent George Read, who had led the investigation, returned to the UK from his new home in Australia. With two other detectives, he faced charges for perjury and conspiracy to pervert the course of justice in relation to the Birmingham Six.

In another part of his address to the jury he exhorted them to put from their minds the fact that Stafford had a criminal record. While it is certainly possible, given Stafford's well publicised criminal career, that some or all the jury were aware of his unsavoury past, up to that point no mention had been made of this and, since he did not go into further details, those who did not know of it must have wondered what precisely his 'record' involved.

The prejudicial implication of these statements paled into insignificance when he went on to create a vivid metaphor to explain away evidence the three had been good friends. Michael vividly remembers that, as he began his summing up the sky above the courtroom's frosted glass roof had darkened and rumbles of thunder filled the air.

In equally thunderous tones O'Connor proclaimed: 'As human beings you will, of course, know that friends are of two types: true friends and false friends,' he told the jury. 'Today is the exact anniversary of the uttering of the famous cry which has rung down through the ages when Julius Caesar lay dying, 'And you Brutus,' whose dagger was in his heart. His friend.' Then pointing an accusing finger directly at Michael, he added: 'Seventy-five years later one greater than Caesar was betrayed by Judas with a kiss. You have seen and heard Michael Luvaglio give his evidence and I am sure that you paid the greatest attention to it. Is he a good actor? Was he a true friend or not?'

'It was like a scene from a film,' says Michael. 'As he said 'Judas' and pointed directly at me, there was a rumble of thunder and a lightning flash. It was very dramatic.'

Later in his summing up the judge discussed the lack of motive: 'It is not necessary, Members of the Jury, in law, for the prosecution to prove a motive, but, of course, the defence quite rightly say that if no motive can be suggested can one be sure that one has got the right men, and you may think that in the story to which you have listened over the last week that there are, or were, things going on among people who were not anxious to have their motives paraded in public. Of course, you will consider it as far as these two men are concerned. There it is. The fact is that no motive is suggested. Some motive has been ruled out. It was not robbery; they did not need Sibbet's money and it was not taken anyway.'

This inference can only be drawn if the accused, neither of whom were short of money, committed the crime.

Our other point of criticism lies in the unbalanced summary of evidence as presented to the jury. The whole feeling and purport of his summing-up cannot be precisely conveyed unless the complete document is reproduced. However, we feel that this is a legitimate criticism which can be fairly illustrated as follows.

Mrs Nora Burnip, as we have seen, was called by the prosecution to say that she heard two sharp cracks at 12.20 am and, looking out of her window, failed to see anything. This hardly made her testimony of any value to the prosecution, since it directly contradicted their theory. But the evidence of this otherwise 'useless' witness could still assist the Crown's case provided that the jury accepted that she had failed, for some reason, to hear three of the shots, and was entirely mistaken as to the time she heard the two.

Alternatively, her evidence could be neutralised so that it didn't damage the prosecution case. The jury might then accept that the two sudden cracks which roused Mrs Burnip from a warm bed were in no way connected with the case. That they had reverberated across the deserted countryside due to some unaccountable phenomenon, unique to the night of January 5.

On the first point Mr Justice O'Connor said: 'Mrs Burnip's recollection, you may think, is based on her normal habits and you may think that she may be quite a long time out in her recollection. You have seen and heard the lady give her evidence, because it could be that lights were put out quite a long time earlier and that really, her recollection is that it was about twenty minutes after the lights were put out, whenever that was, that she heard the cracks. She said that her recollection, to the best of her recollection, that the lights were put out at about midnight, but you see, you may think that that is again of the type of recollection as to time which is based on an uncertain start, and it may be that she is up to half an hour out. If one has gone to bed at half-past-nine would you accurately remember whether you had read for two hours or two and a half hours?'

Whatever the jury may have thought, there was little doubt how Mr Justice O'Connor viewed her evidence. Half an hour back is the critical time. The precise moment when the prosecution says the murder took place. The judge suggested she had made an error. But what basis was there for this suggestion? Mrs Burnip had been asked:
'When you turned your lights out did you see the time on the clock or anything?'
'My husband looked at the time. I did not.'
'How long before the lights went out had he looked at the time?'
'He looked at the time when he put the light out.'

Mr Burnip, although surely interviewed by the police, never gave evidence. Had he placed the time any earlier it is all the more likely that the prosecution would have called him. Mrs Burnip also said that she woke her husband up and they discussed the incident, within seconds of it taking place, and certainly talked about it before she went to the police. Here again we can only assume he would have told her what the time was when the light went off. She was quite specific in her evidence. It was twenty past twelve not, for example, 'sometime between midnight and twelve thirty'.

Where, in any of this testimony, is there anything to justify the judge's conclusion that 'it may be that she is up to half an hour out?'

He might also have remarked upon the fact that the prosecution was trying to have it both ways. They were at great pains to point out that Mrs Burnip would not have seen what took place on the A182 that night because her view was obscured by the haystack near her house. At the same time, if her evidence was accurate, she couldn't have seen anything. According to their theory the murder had taken place half an hour earlier.

Clearly, she can only have been called to support the prosecution case by reinforcing the theory that murder and collision had taken place at the same spot at the same time. Obviously, their contention was that the two sharp cracks were shots, so it was a little strange that Mr Justice O'Connor should have specifically said, 'Mrs Burnip only heard two cracks, which the defence say, were obviously shots.' Then, almost at the end of his summing-up, he returned to her evidence:

'Well, what did she hear? Did she hear the explosion of a gun?'

The logical implication is that if you find her evidence incompatible with the prosecution theory, it is not necessarily contradictory because what she heard might be irrelevant. Equally significant, for the jury, must have been his comments on the credibility and reliability of other witnesses. Where their testimony tended to support the prosecution neither their character nor their testimony was questioned. When defence witnesses or, as frequently happened, prosecution witnesses who cast doubt on the prosecution case, the jury were invited to view their evidence in an entirely different light.

Mr Feather, the bus driver who reported seeing a hand come out of the Mark X's driver's window and wave him on, is a good example of the latter treatment. He made his statement, as we have seen, within a matter of hours of Sibbet's body being found. He had no possible connection with the accused; his evidence was quite definite throughout, in response to the question, under cross-examination, by Mr Scott, for example:

'What was it, as far as you could tell, a man's arm or a woman's arm, or what?'

He replied: 'I have no idea. I would not have seen the arm if it had not been for something white on the lower part of the sleeve. My first impression that it was a police's sleeve you know.'

'Like those white cuffs they wear?'

'Yes, I thought it was one of those.'

Of Mr Feather's testimony, the judge had this to say: 'He told you - he said, 'As I came past it, I saw an arm come out of the window on the offside,' and he undoubtedly thought he was getting a signal for him to overtake. He told you it was snowing at the time; that he had got dipped headlights on and he said that within twenty-four hours he had made a statement to the police. Members of the Jury, you may think, having seen and heard him, that he certainly believes that he received a signal from somebody in that motor car. He said, 'It was only a glance that I noticed the arm. It was just as I was going past.' Well, look at photograph number two. There is the car which is parked in a place where one would not normally expect a car to be. It is, if you look back at photograph number one, not very far from a turning on the other side. You see the turning with the car up the road on the left-hand side, and all sorts of things may pass through a driver's mind. The car is in an unusual situation. It may be that it is going to execute some manoeuvre or another which one anticipates and it is, of course (and those who drive motor cars will know) a most common occurrence that one gets a signal from a motor car if it wants one to go by before it executes some manoeuvre, but you have seen and heard him and it is an important piece of evidence, because if his recollection is trusted on this then it must follow that there was a live man in the car at the same time, and not only a dead body.

You will set that piece of evidence, when you come to consider it, against all the other evidence that there is about the car in this position with its lights on, with the ignition, with the windscreen wipers working as we shall see in one second, because Mr Conroy, the next one who came by, in the opposite direction saw that the windscreen wipers were working, and consider as to whether you think that Mr Feather is honest. No one suggests that he is dishonest and that he is not genuinely telling you what he believes he saw but you will also consider whether he has, and you can accept it as accurate, and if you can, as to what effect it has on the case which I will consider with you in a little while.'

There are three distinct grounds for criticising these remarks.

First the judge said '... it must follow that there was a live man in the car at that time, and not only a dead body'

This shows he accepted the prosecution theory, there is no evidence that Sibbet was dead at that time and was inviting the jury to do the same.

Second, Mr Justice O'Connor went to great lengths to cast doubts on Mr Feather's reliability as a witness. At best this witness was telling the jury what 'he believed he saw', but they would have to consider whether or not it could be accurate. The judge agreed that no one had suggested Mr Feather was a dishonest witness, although immediately before he had invited the jury to consider exactly this proposition.

Finally the jury were told that they had to: 'Set that piece of evidence, when you come to consider it, against all the other evidence that there is about the car in this position with its lights on, with the ignition, with the windscreen wipers working, as we shall see in one second ...'

This is really extraordinary because Mr Feather specifically said that he did not notice whether or not the wipers were working, nor since he approached the vehicle from the rear could he be reasonably expected to. He did, however, say that the lights were on, a fact confirmed by all the other witnesses.

Why then was it necessary to 'set his evidence against' the other testimony? The jury were effectively being told that, if they believed Mr Feather, they would have to disregard the great weight of evidence about the Mark X from the other witnesses.

Others who spoke for the defence received similar treatment. Mrs Dorothy Brady had given evidence about seeing the E-Type outside the

Birdcage Club when she went in with her friend and noticing that the car had been removed when she came out. After summarizing her evidence, the judge said: 'Well, Members of the Jury, as to the first part of her evidence about seeing it there at 12.35, it may be that that is quite right. What about the second part that it was not there at a quarter past one? Is she telling the truth? Is it that she did not notice it and thinks that it was not there, and it is an honest recollection, or, is it a lie, and, if it was not there where was it?'

Mr Robert Anderson and Mrs Gladys Hill had both given evidence about seeing the E-Type outside Luvaglio's house in Chelsea Grove. Anderson was quite definite about what he had seen and when he had seen it. He remained unshaken under cross-examination and the prosecution never suggested he was lying. His evidence, did however, give rise to a number of doubts in the mind of Mr Justice O'Connor: 'Is he mistaken about the time without wishing to in any way deliberately do so? Could it be that he spent rather more than ten minutes after the television had stopped before he went to put his car away? Could it be that there is another red car which he saw, he says not, which he mistook? Could it be that he is not telling you the truth?'

Mrs Hill had actually asked her daughter what the time was just before they left the club where they were having a meal. She knew therefore that it was just before midnight that they started for home and she estimates as we have seen in an earlier chapter, that the walk takes her between five and seven minutes. This is, after all, a journey she does twice a day and it is reasonable to suppose that she would know fairly accurately how long it took. She had given her evidence to an agent employed by the defence within a few days, when these facts were fresh in her mind.

Mr Justice O'Connor still felt it reasonable to propose that 'she may be out by twenty or twenty-five minutes.' There are, of course, no grounds for suggesting that since these witnesses are so unreliable as to the time their testimony should be disregarded. The timetable which Stafford and Luvaglio would have had to follow in order to carry out the killing, according to the prosecution theory, was so tight that the E-Type could not have been outside Chelsea Grove at any other time that evening.

The police made their test run in perfect conditions allowing only a reasonable minimum period for carrying out the various activities they envisaged. They also drove a far more easily handled Mark X rather than an E-Type. Even so they arrived at the Birdcage at 12.31 am when the bulk of evidence suggests that Stafford and Luvaglio got there just after 12.20 am.

What grounds can there possibly be for Mr Justice O'Connor's suggestion: 'Maybe there is time to go to Chelsea Grove and still be at the Birdcage round about half past twelve'.

While considering the timetable of events that night, let us look at the way in which the evidence of the three women at Westmorland Rise, Selena Jones, Pat Burgess and Lilian Bunker, was treated in the summing-up. As we have already seen they all contradicted police evidence that Stafford and Luvaglio had left the house at eleven o'clock which would have made a meeting with Sibbet some time before 11.30 pm at least a possibility.

Is their recollection an accurate one? Is their recollection an honest one, or is there some very good reason for trying to account for where Stafford and Luvaglio really were at about a quarter to twelve, ten to twelve, twelve o'clock?

The evidence of Selena Jones and Pat Burgess is, of course, open to suspicion, although, as we said in previously, it is hard to see what incentive Lilian Bunker had to lie and the judge made no reference to her testimony. In fact, the whole question of this departure time seems very strange. Superintendent Kell and Detective Superintendent Mitchell claim that both Stafford and Luvaglio told them, in separate interviews, they had left home at eleven o'clock. This they vehemently deny as does Stafford's solicitor Mr Graham Andrews, who was present during the interview. The prosecution suggested the Westmorland Rise witnesses were lying but that Stafford and Luvaglio during that first interview were telling the truth.

Is this in any way logical?

Suppose Stafford and Luvaglio had, indeed, murdered Sibbet. In this event, as we have already pointed out, they would have known what time he died and been careful to establish an alibi to account for their movements over that period. Clearly, they would have planned their story during the hours following the murder before returning home to instruct the three women what they should say if questioned by the police. They would have hammered home to them that they had left the house no earlier than 11.30 pm. Yet, the moment they are interviewed by the police both men had, apparently, stated a departure time of eleven o'clock. This, in the full knowledge, it would be flatly denied by the three women. Mr Justice O'Connor did not mention this point, although he dealt at some length with these two interviews. Because the whole case hinges on the time Dennis and Michael left Peterlee to drive to Newcastle is so important, let's take a closer look at how the judge dealt with it in his summing up.

Regarding the time stated in the initial police interviews he had this to say: 'Later on, that day [5 January] there took place the interview with the police officers and a number of criticisms are made, perfectly properly. It is common ground that when Luvaglio who was the first to be interviewed, was seen by the two police officers, Kell and Mitchell. Superintendent Kell saw Luvaglio first in an interview which began apparently at 12.25 am the morning of the sixth of January. Remember that they had been asked to come to the police station; that they had both gone to bed in Westmorland Rise and had to get up and get dressed, and Luvaglio told the police officers for all practical purposes the same story he has told you.

I am not going to go through the history of the trip to Jamaica [sic. He meant

Majorca] and picking up the car. When Stafford in his turn was seen he had his solicitor present and he said that - and he is perfectly entitled to do this and do not hold it against him at all - that he did not wish to make a statement but that he was prepared to answer questions, and effectively, what the police officers wanted to know was: 'What were your movements during the fourth of January and the night of the fourth/fifth?' They got from each of the men separately an accurate timetable as far as the men were concerned to which they have sworn, but there are two discrepancies. The police officers say that each said that they had left Peterlee at about 11 pm and travelled to Chelsea Grove, expecting a call to arrive at Chelsea Grove between midnight and 12.15 a.m. 'Waited for a while. Gone to the Birdcage.'

That was what Luvaglio is alleged to have told the police. Stafford, according to the police officer's note and recollection, said they left Peterlee at about 11 pm and driven to Chelsea Grove, where they were expecting a call from Vincent. They had then gone on to the Birdcage Club arriving between 12.30 and 12.40.

Of these statements O'Connor commented: 'Each has said 'Well, the police have got eleven o'clock wrong, we said eleven thirty,' and they point out - it has been pointed out on their behalf - that the interviews were fairly long ones and that not everything which was said got recorded. You have heard the police officers invited to apply their minds as to whether a television programme was mentioned; as to whether something was spilt on the note, to which they said 'no'. They have got no recollection of that.

You have heard the criticism made by saying, 'Well, the police officers were really not prepared to concede anything other than what was in Mr Mitchell's notes,' and you have heard the last witness of all, Stafford's solicitor, who, you will remember, did not make a note of his own at all, say to you [that was Mr Andrews] that it was question and answer and that his recollection was that Stafford had said he left Peterlee about eleven thirty and qualified his reasons by referring to a film on the television and then wrestling and the name of the film mentioned was 'What Lola Wants'. The police officers said they had no recollection of that.

The other dispute is that, Mr Andrew's recollection was that Stafford told the police officers that they had arrived at Chelsea Grove about midnight and that they had arrived at the Birdcage Cafe about...the Birdcage Club... about twelve thirty.

Members of the Jury, it may or may not be important. The police officers, you may think, were doing their best to getting down the times. They are criticised by saying, 'Well, when you were told eleven o'clock and not outside Chelsea Grove until twelve or just after didn't you ask why on earth it had taken an hour', and he told you that they were really trying to get down a story, or rather Mitchell was.

I will remind you about it. He said that he did not remember having any tea while the interview was going on and that he thought that he had made a full note of his replies, and, 'I am sure Stafford did not mention television or wrestling', and he stuck to saying that he got it down correctly. He was asked about the reason that they had taken the E-Type and there was the answer that the heater in the big estate car did not work.

Mr Mitchell said, 'I am confident he did not say the heater in the car did not work,' and he denied that there was that piece of conversation with Stafford, saying it would take half an hour and Kell saying, 'What, in an E-Type?' And the reply, 'I have never had a ticket for speeding.'

These matters were all put to the police officers and the purpose of those questions and the importance of them is whether the original timetable, which was told to the police, that vital part, was the departure at eleven or half past.

Well, Members of the Jury, it may or may not matter. Peterlee is not terribly far from Hetton-Le-Hole. It is not many miles and the first sight of the two cars in convoy is not until sometime shortly before, you may think, a quarter to one, if Mr Johnson's observation was accurate, the Overman who looked at his watch.

At this point Mr Dean rose hastily to his feet: 'I think your Lordship means a quarter to twelve.'

'Sorry, I am very much obliged, a quarter to twelve, so you are left to consider as to whether they have tried to change their story, or, whether in the course of taking down the timings, which was the thing the police officers were interested in, Mitchell and Kell made the same mistake with both men. There is, of course, a third alternative.'

It is very difficult to reconcile the two comments Mr Justice O'Connor made about the departure time from Peterlee. It cannot, at the same time, be 'vital' and something which 'may or may not matter'. Here again it seems that the jury were being offered a convenient alternative if they found the prosecution evidence as to the time of departure unsatisfactory. Should they decide that the men had left at eleven thirty, that the police officers were in error for whatever reasons, they could still accept the prosecution theory as a whole.

We have already noted the brevity of the notes taken by Detective Superintendent Mitchell during the interviews which Superintendent Kell had with the accused. For an interview with Stafford of seventy-five minutes without a break the note occupied only four columns of writing on one side of a piece of paper and took a total of seven and a half minutes to read to the court. The interview with Michael Luvaglio lasted fifty-five minutes and required only one sheet of foolscap paper to record it. Both officers, giving evidence, insisted throughout that a full record had been kept of everything said by the accused, and vehemently denied anything, however trivial, which was not included in the notes. As Superintendent Kell told Mr Lyons under cross-examination: 'Would you agree that Mr Stafford told you a good deal more than you have

read out of your notebook?'
'No, Sir.'
'That is correct is it?'
'No, Sir.'
'No, well did he tell you more than you have read out?'
'He may have repeated himself on certain events but did not tell us more.'
'Are you suggesting that Mr Mitchell was able to take down the substance of everything he said?'
'I would say that he did. Sir, yes.'
Detective Superintendent Mitchell was equally positive:
'There were many more questions and answers, perhaps of a subsidiary nature, but many more questions and answers than the answers you have written down?' suggested Mr Lyons.
'Oh, no, I would not agree with you, Sir.'
'You say that you have written down everything that was said by Mr Stafford.'
'I would say very much all that was said, Sir.'
        Within seconds he was proved wrong. About half an hour earlier Superintendent Kell had confirmed that Stafford told him that the car was garaged overnight at Peterlee. Mr Lyons asked Mitchell:
'Did he tell you that he put the E-Type in his garage at his home?'
'I do not recall him saying that. Sir.'
'Well, what do you think about that?'
'Well, I don't think it is on the note, Sir.'
'I know it is not on the note, so is this the position...?'
'Well, if he had said it, it would be on the note, Sir.'
        There were many other matters, of no great significance in themselves which, it was put to the police officers, came up during the first interviews. These included the fact that the television programmes that night were mentioned, and that Stafford explained he hadn't locked the E-Type outside the Birdcage Club because, having a soft top, it could so easily be slashed open to be stolen. This last remark was particularly remembered by the solicitor Graham Andrews, because he had had a convertible car stolen in just this way.
        Kell and Mitchell denied that anything of this nature had been said, even though it made not the slightest difference to the value of the answers. It seems strange indeed that Mr Andrews, a former councillor and partner in a local firm of solicitors, should take it into his head to invent such pointless chit-chat. It was also suggested to both police officers that they should surely have been surprised at the statement, attributed to both men, that the journey from Peterlee to Newcastle should have taken between one and one and a quarter hours. Mr Dean asked Kell:
'I want to ask you about the next time, because the next time referred to in your note is that they talked to Stafford and Selena Jones until about eleven p.m. when he and Stafford left Peterlee in the red E-Type Jaguar?'

'Yes, Sir.'
'Now, that ought to be eleven thirty?'
'No, Sir.'
'I will tell you why I ask you this. Luvaglio told you that he arrived at Chelsea Grove, which is his home in Newcastle, between twelve midnight and twelve fifteen?'
'Yes, Sir.'
'You know that it does not take an hour or an hour and a quarter to drive from Peterlee to Chelsea Grove?'
'I do indeed.'
'And I suggest, if he had told you he had left Peterlee at eleven and not arrived at Chelsea Grove until twelve you would have wanted to know what he was doing during that hour?'
'No, Sir. I did not ask him.'
Detective Superintendent Mitchell agreed this point had occurred to him and told Mr Dean: 'You ask, Sir, 'did it surprise me? ... well, yes, yes, it did occur to me.'
'Did you say you were making those very inquiries? Did you say why did it take you so long?'
'I did not say anything. Superintendent Kell was asking the questions.'
Apparently when they started the one-and-a-quarter-hour interview with Dennis Stafford both officers had already realised that the eleven o'clock departure time was irreconcilable with an arrival at Newcastle over an hour later. Yet when Stafford repeated this statement in the course of that long interview neither made any comment.'
Mr Lyons suggested to Superintendent Kell that in fact this point had already been raised and asked: 'You asked how long the drive took and the answer was 'about half an hour'. You asked, 'In an E-Type?' Answer: 'Well I have never had a ticket for speeding and the roads were icy as well.'
'No, Sir.'
Graham Andrews was also asked about this and confirmed that Stafford had told the officers that he left Peterlee at about 11.30 p.m. At times the officers' insistence that anything not specifically recorded in Detective Superintendent Mitchell's notes was sheer invention on the part of the accused and Stafford's solicitor became a little more than dogmatic. As this exchange between Mr Lyons and Detective Superintendent Mitchell illustrates:
'At one stage did you not tell him when your birthday was, for instance?'
'Told him what, Sir?'
'When your birthday was?'
'Oh, no, certainly not.'
'Is your birthday by any chance in July?'
'No, it isn't.'
'What month?'
'June.'

'Wasn't there a reference to your coming under the Cancer sign of the Zodiac?'
'I don't recall that.'
'Do you come under that sign of the Zodiac?'
'I have no idea.'
'From the twenty-second of June to the twenty-second July?'
'I have no idea.'
'When is your birthday?'
'The twenty-eighth of June.'
'That does come under the sign?'
'I don't know, Sir.'
'Wasn't there a discussion between Stafford, who is interested in astrology...?'
'Between whom?'
'Between you and Mr Stafford?'
'I certainly do not recall it.'
'And you gave him your birthday and he said you come under Cancer?'
'This was during the interview?'
'Either during or at the end of it?'
'There was some reference after three am, after the interview had been concluded.'
'This was said but it was after the interview?'
'Oh, yes. yes. There were some jovial remarks by Stafford.'
'Did you, in fact, at that time, tell him when your birthday was?'
'Well, I certainly do not recall it, it is possible I might have.'

Clearly, there is a very substantial conflict between these two officer's versions of those initial interviews and the defence version based on the recollections of Stafford, Luvaglio and Graham Andrews. Any experienced police officer would appreciate how vitally important it was to establish that his record of the interviews was entirely accurate, since once faulted even on a minor matter its reliability on crucial points might also become questionable.

This whole argument could have been avoided had Mr Graham Andrews either taken his own notes, or perhaps better, read and authenticated the officer's record. However, he didn't, and later told the court that he felt this was regrettable but considered that the accuracy of a Detective Superintendent could be relied upon.

We can only leave it to you to decide which of these versions are most likely to reflect the truth, but suggest that before you do so, try carrying out this simple exercise. Recount to yourself, slowly but in no great detail, the significant events of the past forty-eight hours to see how long this takes? Most people who have done so find they are able to manage it in well under an hour-and-a-quarter!

At the start of his summing-up Mr Justice O'Connor told the jury:
'If you are left in any reasonable doubt you do not hesitate to acquit. Remember that a reasonable doubt is one for which you could give reasons if you were

asked.'

Surely this means that the jury were expected to provide reasons why Stafford and Luvaglio should be acquitted, a definition that was later roundly criticised by the Appeal Court.

Shortly before 2.17 pm, on 15 March, Mr Justice O'Connor concluded with this stricture to the jury: 'I have explained the burden of proof to you, and, Members of Jury, let me finish by saying that it is very important that people who are not proved to be guilty should not be convicted, but it is equally important that those who are proved to be guilty are convicted. I do not think I can help you further in this case.'

The jury retired, returning a little over an hour later to ask for copies of statements made by two witnesses. The judge was obliged to rule that these could not be made available, since they were not exhibits, and the jury once again left the court.

At 5.10 pm they returned. The Clerk of Assize rose and faced them: 'Members of the Jury, who shall speak as your foreman? Mr Foreman, will you stand up please and answer the following questions on behalf of the jury. Members of the Jury, are you agreed upon your verdict?'

'We are Sir.'

'Do you find Michael Luvaglio guilty or not guilty of murder?'

'Guilty.'

'Do you find Dennis Stafford guilty or not guilty of murder?'

'Guilty.'

'And are those the verdicts of you all?'

'Those are the verdicts of us all.'

Chapter Thirteen: House of Cards

'It is a question of whether the Prosecution case has been sufficiently knocked about, if I may use that expression, to make it impossible to say that the verdict remains safe and satisfactory.' Lord Chief Justice Widgery

Perhaps, after considering all the evidence we have presented, you believe the life sentences handed down to Dennis and Michael were richly deserved. Maybe you even feel they should have hanged for such a cold-blooded capital murder. This might well have happened had they been convicted before November 1965.

If this is your judgement you have accepted, in whole or in large part, each of the twelve components in the prosecution's house of cards. If one card fails, then the entire structure falls. The evidential cards making up their case can be summarised as follows:

1. The accused left Peterlee around 11pm on the night of January 4.
2. They met Sibbet, driving alone in his Mark X, on the B1284 shortly before 11.30 pm.
3. The E-Type and the Mark X continued in convoy along the A182 passing through South Hetton, for the first time that night, between 11.42 and 11.46 pm.
4. The only people involved were Dennis Stafford and Michael Luvaglio. They had no accomplices.
5. The collision and murder occurred, within a minute or so of 11.50 pm, opposite West Moor Farm.
6. Cyclist James Golden, although only yards from the murder scene, neither saw nor heard anything out of the ordinary.
7. The E-Type and Mark X stopped briefly in Pesspool Lane where the saloon was cleaned out. Debris, including cigarette butts, was left by the roadside.
8. The cars travelled in a wide circle, ending up back on the A182 and returning to South Hetton where the Mark X overheated, stalled and was abandoned by Pesspool Bridge.
9. The damaged E-Type drove directly to the Birdcage Club where it had arrived between 12.20 and 12.30 am.
10. It was never parked outside Chelsea Grove.
11. The damaged E-Type was outside the Piccadilly Club, from between 12.20 and 12.30 until well after 2 am.
12. The Mark X had damage to the front end, a shot out rear window and the corpse of Angus Stewart Sibbet on the back seat from 11.50 onward.

Let's review each of these twelve key elements on the prosecution case in turn.

1. The accused left Peterlee well before 11.30 pm on the night of January 4.
2. They met Sibbet, driving alone in his Mark X, on the B1284 shortly before 11.30 pm.
3. The E-Type and the Mark X drove in convoy along the A182 passing through South Hetton between 11.42 and 11.46 pm.

The only evidence the prosecution called to establish that the accused left earlier than 11.30 pm, came from Kell and Mitchell. The detectives claim that Michael and Dennis stated, independently and during fairly friendly interviews, they had left the house at 11 pm and made no attempt to correct themselves. They referred to notes made during the 'question and answer' sessions early in the morning of 6 January and to the evidence of Stafford's neighbour Mr Wells. He could only say that he saw the E-Type turned around in the cul-de-sac and Stafford standing by the gate of 109 Westmorland Rise. He didn't see the car drive away, and had no idea of the actual time of departure but thinks what he saw took place between 11.05 and 11.35 pm.

As we have already pointed out, both strongly deny they gave their departure time as 11pm Stafford this is supported in his denial by his solicitor, Graham Andrews. Both men knew the drive from Peterlee to Newcastle takes thirty minutes and, had they murdered Sibbet, would also have known how vital in was to account for their movements during that period. It is also reasonable to assume that much of their time, between the murder and their arrest, was taken up ensuring they and their Westmorland Rise witnesses gave a consistent account of the events that evening.

At Stafford's house three witnesses supported a much later departure time. This they did consistently, despite the fact that, at any time, the police might have produced evidence which would lay them open to a conviction for perjury and conspiracy to pervert the course of justice.

The same arguments apply to the cars driving in convoy down the A 182. Unless they left Westmorland Rise far earlier than they, and their witnesses, say, it couldn't have been their E-Type which Mr Knight saw pull out from his right at about 11.35 pm, or the miners watched driving through South Hetton, five to ten minutes later.

Accept the evidence of Selena Jones, Pat Burgess, Lilian Bunker, solicitor Graham Andrews, Dennis Stafford and Michael Luvaglio and the prosecution fails.

4. The only people involved in the murder were Dennis Stafford and Michael Luvaglio. There had no accomplices.

This conflicts with the finding of blood, belonging to neither Dennis nor Michael on the transmission well of the Mark X and another blood stain, belonging to the same, fairly common, group of Sibbet on the page of a telephone directory in the South Hetton phone box. As we will explain in the final chapter, it is also contradicted by an eye-witness statement from a garage worker.

Could Dennis and Michael have been assisted by a third, never identified accomplice? This was what Mr Justice O'Connor suggested in his summing-up:

'What about the blood on Stafford's motor car - I am sorry, on Sibbet's motor car on the transmission housing. How did it get there? Was it part of that night's work? Was there another person in the murdering gang? Has it got some wholly different explanation? The only thing that you can be certain of is that it does not implicate Stafford and Luvaglio.'

Even had the bloodstain not done so, the phrase 'another person in the murdering gang' can hardly to have helped the accused. In our view the presence of a third man explains nothing. Surely the function of an accomplice is to assist the murderers. In this case he who must have had a third vehicle and could have removed Sibbet's body to ensure it was not found for several days, making it almost impossible to estimate the time of death. He could have removed the E-Type from outside the Birdcage Club and left it miles away or got it repaired surreptitiously. An accomplice does not explain James Golden's evidence, nor Tom Feather's, nor any of the witnesses at Peterlee, those who saw the E-Type at Chelsea Grove, nor the evidence of any of the miners who passed the Mark X that night.

If we believe that Dennis and Michael are innocent, then clearly some other person or persons shot Sibbet. Far from being accomplices these killers did all they could to implicate the accused. As we have mentioned, fresh blood was found on the Mark X's transmission tunnel, which matched neither of the accused nor the victim.

Police Constable Ainsworth reported seeing a Jaguar saloon and a red Mini travelling in convoy.

Accept that the unidentified blood stain indicates the presence of a third killer and the prosecution fails.

5.   The collision and murder occurred, within a minute or so of 11.50 pm, on the A182 opposite West Moor Farm.

The police claimed Sibbet's shooting occurred opposite West Moor Farm at 11.50 pm or very shortly before or after that time. There is no defence evidence about this, and we can only rely on the credibility of the two prosecution witnesses.

Farmer's wife Nora Burnip, who maintained throughout that the two sharp cracks she heard occurred no earlier than 12.20 am. She was lying awake in bed and the sounds were so strange and unexpected that she immediately awoke her husband and got up to try and see what had caused them. If they were indeed shots, they must surely have been connected with the murder, so why did she hear only two and not five, and why was it half an hour after the shots were actually fired, assuming again the prosecution theory is correct? The only alternative is that these cracks were caused by some totally unrelated and mysterious phenomenon which never occurred before or after that night.

If this is so, how was it that Mr and Mrs Burnip sitting up in bed reading were unable to hear at, in the silence of deserted countryside, at a distance of 260 yards and with the wind blowing any sounds towards their windows, a squeal of brakes, a loud collision and five gun shots fired from an automatic pistol which could not be fitted with a silencer. Accept the evidence of Nora Burnip and the prosecution fails.

6.   Cyclist James Golden, who would have been only yards from the scene if the policy theory is correct, neither saw nor heard anything out of the ordinary.

If we combine his slowest possible cycling speed with the murderers' fastest time, he would still have been only 128 yards away when the cars collided, and only a few yards further on when the shots were fired. How could he have failed to hear them? How could he, peddling down that long, straight, stretch of road have been unaware of the powerful headlamps of two fast cars when he must have been cycling within their throw of light?

If, that night, he had cycled as fast as the private detective timed him under worse conditions, and if the killers took half the four minutes which the police allowed, then he would have cycled past them at the precise moment Sibbet was being gunned down.

When the cars overtook him, he noticed their speed, their make, the order in which they were travelling and the distance between them. Could he, then, have failed to notice if the rear lights of the sports car had been smashed and were glaring white? Accept the evidence of James Golden and the prosecution fails.

7.   The E-Type and Mark X stopped briefly in Pesspool Lane where the saloon was cleaned and debris, including cigarette butts, left by the roadside.

Had the two cars turned right into Pesspool Lane, immediately after the murder, they must have been seen doing so by James Golden. Despite what Chief Superintendent Kell told the court, on oath, it is perfectly possible to see the junction at any distance Golden would have been away from it. At night, on a lonely and otherwise deserted road he could hardly have missed them. Accept the findings of an experienced Chartered Surveyor and the evidence of photographs taken for this book, and the prosecution fails.

8.   The cars travelled in a wide circle to South Hetton where the Mark X overheated, stalled and was abandoned.

We have dealt at length with the conflicting evidence regarding the condition of the Mark X's engine and the anonymous allegation a police officer deliberately ran the engine dry to justify the stall theory. There is the curious damage to the Mark X radiator. Two small holes which apparently could not have been due to the collision, but which could, all the experts agreed, have been deliberately punched with a screwdriver or a similar instrument. Then there is the anonymous letter claiming a police office had deliberately run the car's engine without water in the radiator until it seized.

Why retrace your route down the A182 when the incriminating Mark X could have been abandoned, not under a bright streetlamp on a busy main road, but in the darkness and seclusion of far less used Pesspool Lane? The only explanation for this bizarre drive was provided, not by the prosecution, but by Mr Justice O'Connor. He suggested they might have been on their way to the sea, some six miles away, where they would dump the body. This despite the fact there was no evidence they had a boat and that the time involved in doing so would destroy any alibi they might have had.

Accept the findings of Jaguar engineer George Bowman and the contents of the letter and the prosecution fails.

9.   The E-Type drove directly to the Birdcage Club where it had arrived between 12.20 and 12.30 am.

10. It was never parked outside Chelsea Grove and never left undamaged when parked outside the Birdcage Club.

It is also necessary to accept the two men could never have stopped in Chelsea Grove because there simply was not time to do so. This means rejecting the evidence of Mrs Hill, Pat Morgan and Mr Anderson, Michael's neighbours, who told the court they had seen the sports car outside his home at about 12.05 am. We have already explained why there is very little chance that they were mistaken about the night because the E-Type had been at the Wheatsheaf under lock and key since before Christmas and was in police custody from the evening of 5 January onwards. The prosecution suggested that they might have been confused about the time, but it is strange that they should both make the same mistake. In any event this is irrelevant. No matter how fast an E-Type can travel it cannot be in two places at once.

They had no apparent motive for lying and, had they been prepared to commit perjury their lies could have been far more helpful to the defence.

Accept the evidence of these witnesses and the prosecution fails.

11. The damaged E-Type was parked outside the Piccadilly Club, from between 12.20 and 12.30 until well after 2 am.

There is, of course, no prosecution evidence that it was in a damaged condition when it arrived, nor that it remained in the same position. Indeed, it was a prosecution witness, club doorman Matthew Dean, who suggested that it had been moved. It appeared to him from tyre tracks in the snow that it had been pushed forward. As the accused could not have left the club without being seen by Dean, they obviously didn't move it.

Dorothy Brady, a witness with good reason to identify and remember the presence of Vince Landa's car, testified it was there when she arrived. She failed to notice whether or not the lights were on, which perhaps she might have done more readily if the rear lights had been glowing white. On leaving the club she said that the car was no longer there. Here again it is unlikely she was mistaken about the date, nor is there any apparent reason why she should be mistaken in her observation. We are again left with the possibility that she is lying, in which case here is another ordinary person with only a tenuous connection to the accused prepared to perjure themselves on their behalf.

So far as the E-Type is concerned, there is the evidence of Dorothy Brady that it was removed whilst Stafford and Luvaglio were in the club. Doorkeeper Matthew Dean testified that the car had, apparently, been moved from its original parking position. There is also the damage to the rear of the E-Type which cannot be explained by the prosecution theory of two collisions between the cars, and the strange shattering of the rear light lenses on both sides of the vehicle. Engineer George Bowman considered that this could only be explained by a deliberate action, such as striking the lights with a hammer.

Was another E-Type used by the killers in a, successful, attempt to throw very strong suspicion either on Stafford and Luvaglio, or possibly on Vince Landa? The killer or killers may not have realised he had gone back to Majorca and lent Dennis and Michael his car? Driving these two expensive and distinctive vehicles, nose to tail, slowly through South Hetton seems more calculated to attract than avoid attention.

Was the E-Type then removed from outside the Birdcage Club and driven into a deliberate collision with the Mark X along the A182 road? Was the Mark X driven back into Newcastle, a collision staged outside or near the club, and some of the debris collected and scattered along the A182? It was after all only the rear light lenses on the A182 which formed the link, and no one seems to have seen the Mark X between 12.50 and 1.50 am.

Alternatively, perhaps as the E-Type stood outside the Birdcage Club, in a back street, the rear lights broken with a hammer, and after Stafford and Luvaglio returned it to Westmorland Rise, sometime after 3 am, it was taken and a collision staged with the Mark X along the A182. Such a later collision is the only way in which the miners' evidence about lack of damage at 2.30 am can be explained.

We will justify these speculations more fully in the final chapter. But accept the evidence of Matthew Dean and Dorothy Brady and the prosecution fails.

12. The Mark X had damage to the front end, a shot out rear window and the corpse of Angus Stewart Sibbet on the back seat from 11.50 onward.

According to the police the Mark X must have been at the bridge by 12.10. Yet confectioner Mauro Ferri drove through South Hetton at this time and saw no car there. We must remember that what made all the other witnesses remember the car standing there was that it was badly parked.

Could Mauro Ferri have failed to see it?

At 12.45 am, bus driver Tom Feather drove up behind the Mark X and then pulled out to overtake it, encouraged by a hand which emerged from one of the off-side windows, presumably the driving window, and beckoned him on.

He remembers the white cuff, it struck him at the time as being like a policeman's, and he has no doubt whatsoever about what he saw.

Can Mr Feather have imagined this?

At 1.50 am, miner Alan Wood walked up to the saloon on his way home from work and stopped to admire the vehicle, wondering why it was parked there. He leaned across the bonnet and could feel the heat coming up from the engine, and noticed footprints in the freshly fallen snow, leading away from the car. He couldn't see anybody in the car, and didn't notice any sign of damage to the vehicle.

About 2.25 am, four miners on their way to work walked past the car, heading north towards the colliery. Two of them had to step off the pavement and walk past the car's offside. Both stated all its windows were intact. Surely if one had been smashed and the other wound down, they would have noticed this, glanced into the vehicle and observed Sibbet's white shirt reflecting light from the near-by sodium lamp. All them searched for an explanation for the presence of this expensive saloon in such an incongruous place at such an odd time. Yet apparently none of them could see the broken headlights and extensive damage to the bodywork which would provide the most obvious of explanations.

The jury heard only the evidence of Thomas Purvis, so were unable properly to appreciate or consider the full impact of this evidence. Why was this? According to Dennis Stafford and the appeal transcript, these witnesses were in fact known to the defence, but not called because it was felt that since the accused had an alibi from midnight onwards until 4 am (Dr Ennis's original murder period) the events after midnight were unimportant. When their statements were taken, the only striking feature of their evidence was that they noticed nothing unusual about the car. At the time the defence could not have appreciated just how crucial this would turn out to be.

Accept the evidence of Mauro Ferri, Thom Feather, Alan Wood, James Bradbury, Thomas Purvis, Alexander Howie and Stanley Simpson, or any one of them, and the prosecution fails.

Are Selena Jones, Pat Burgess, Lilian Bunker, Gladys Hill, Robert Anderson, Graham Andrews, Dorothy Brady, Mauro Ferri, Thomas Feather, Alan Wood, Thomas Purvis, Alexander Howie, Stanley Simpson, James Bradbury, James Golden, Nora Burnip and Matthew Dean, all deliberately lying or utterly mistaken?

In which case, you can only conclude that Michael Luvaglio, an intelligent young man with no police record, a Catholic who eschewed violence and avoided trouble whenever he could, was a cold-blood professional killer. A merciless gunman capable of shooting dead his best friend at close range one moment and relaxing, chatting, eating and drinking, in a nightclub less than an hour later.

Even the police did not really believe he was involved, if an offer made to his solicitor, Harry Mincoff is anything to go by. In the 'seventies, Mincoff a highly respected Newcastle lawyer described, on record, how he had been approached by Chief Superintendent Kell during the trial. Kell told him he did not believe his client had anything to do with the murder and offered an easy way out. All he had to do was make a statement saying he and Dennis were not together during the early part of that night he could walk free from the court.' A similar offer was made to Michael, some years later, when he was in Wakefield prison. On both occasions he turned the offer down flat. 'It simply would not have been true,' the Michael told us. 'Dennis and I were together the whole of that night, and I am not prepared to lie about it.'

Years later, Mincoff commented on the conviction: 'After all this time I'm still convinced Luvaglio was innocent. My own view is that it was a contract killing carried out by hitmen from outside the region. At that time the London villains such as the Krays were trying to muscle into the lucrative nightclub scene in Newcastle.'

We share this opinion and, in the penultimate chapter, will describe one possible scenario for what happened that bitterly cold January night more than half a century ago.

Other Failings in the Prosecution Case
It was more than remarkable that no forensic scientific links were found between either of the accused, the dead man, the Mark X or the crime scene. Nor was there anything at the crime scene to indicate their presence. This despite the vast amounts of material, glass, plastic, grass, mud etc, examined.

What the police did find, although it was never mentioned in court or disclosed to the defence, was a box of foreign made cigars on the dashboard of the Mark X. Michael, Dennis and Sibbet smoked only cigarettes. Who left the box in Sibbet's car? If the police tested the box for fingerprints, which they presumably did, no reference was made to them in court, nor were the defence lawyers made aware of them.

Also suppressed were fingerprints found on the edges of both rear doors. That part of the door which might be grasped when opening the doors to their widest, as for example when manoeuvring a body onto the rear seat. The police established, but never mentioned, the fact that these prints belonged to neither Dennis or Michael.

The medical evidence, as interpreted by Professor Francis Camps, indicates that the most probable time of death was 1.30 am. Only by accepting the minimum possible cooling rate can the prosecution's time for the murder be correct.

It is very difficult to see how the damage to the cars could have resulted from the accidental collisions envisaged by the police. If Mr Bowman's criticisms are valid, and he is correct in deciding there must have been three collisions, then here again the reconstruction of events according to the prosecution has to be incorrect.

The curious position of the five cartridge cases must give rise to at least a passing doubt that all the shots were fired from the same spot.

Finally, we come to the psychology of the two alleged professional gunmen.

If the prosecution is correct, these 'hitmen' were so incompetent they failed to provide themselves with an alibi. So indifferent to the consequences of their actions they drove to the murder in an eye-catching sports car belonging to the chairman of a company with which they were closely associated. So arrogant they arranged a rendezvous with their victim in such a way they had to drive in convoy with him for miles along a busy and, in parts, well lit, main road. Such inept shots they missed their victim twice, despite firing from only feet away. So reckless they drove Sibbet's damaged saloon, with his body in the back, in company with an E-Type's whose smashed rear light made it more noticeable than usual, in a Mark X any experienced driver would have realised was about to stall. Engineers have confirmed that long before the vehicle came to a halt near Pesspool Bridge, the engine would have given clear signs of overheating.

Who Commits Murder?

Murder is typically motivated by just three things: passion, greed or fear.

This was clearly a crime neither of passion nor of greed. Sibbet's wallet and expensive watch where found, untouched, on his corpse. So far as anybody knew neither of the accused had any reason to fear him. While Angus was stealing large sums of cash each week, from Vince Landa's company, much of it was with his full knowledge and the business remained immensely profitable. Had it been felt Sibbet's thievery had reached unacceptable proportions, perfectly good and legal remedies were available. Sibbet could have been dismissed and made the subject of civil or criminal proceedings.

Was Sibbet brutally killed as a warning to others who might be tempted to steal? This is only likely if you believe Social Club Services, a financially successful and well-run company, was an organisation where dishonest employees were brutally gunned down.

Despite the lack of convincing motive and the glaring weakness and inconsistencies we have described, you may still feel that the prosecution case stands. After all real-life murder bears little relation to a neatly plotted detective story. Not everything can be expected to fit into a pigeon-hole. But look again at the twelve essential elements in the prosecution's jigsaw puzzle to understand what this acceptance implies and what evidence must be rejected.

Let us for one moment assume that they are innocent. Place yourself in the shoes of these two young men, whose lives were destroyed. Imagine that, one night, your parked car is damaged in a mysterious collision.

The following night you are taken from your bed to a police interview room. They inform you they are investigating the murder of a close friend. You honestly outline your movements over the previous forty-eight hours. What you say is confirmed by everybody in a position to do so, including virtual strangers. You readily agree the police can check every item of your clothing, for you know there can be nothing to connect you with the messy crime scene - and of course there is not. You know you had no motive to kill your friend, and of course none is proved.

The weeks spent on remand in a high security prison are a nightmare, but you are still confident that you and the many other defence witnesses will not be dismissed as idiots or liars. But indeed, that is precisely what happened.

In any trial it is the role of defence lawyers to bring weaknesses and inconsistencies in the prosecution's case to a jury's attention. It is not their job to provide an alternative theory as to how the crime took place or who may have committed it.

In the final chapter we will describe what our investigations have revealed about the events on that night and offer three different scenarios for the shooting dead of Angus Sibbet.

The first is that he was murdered on orders of fruit machine rivals Ronnie and Reggie Kray. We name and provide an identikit portrait of the likely hitman, created, by a former Scotland Yard artist, from the eye-witness testimony of a garage mechanic who met him the morning after the murder.

Our second scenario looks at possible involvement by Vince Landa. A killing he ordered to punish Sibbet for stealing from his company and for his blackmail attempt a few years earlier.

Finally, we explore the likelihood of a third man or men. A professional killer hired by a rival gambling organisation to take revenge on Sibbet for stealing from their machines and bring down Vince Landa's vice like grip on gambling in the North-East.

Chapter Fourteen: The Man Who Shot Angus Sibbet?

'I can't say I was affected in any way by their deaths. They had no impact on me. There's no point dancing on their graves.' Albert Donoghue, Reggie Kray's right-hand man.

One of the problems confronting anyone setting out to discover who murdered Angus that freezing January night, is the conflicting eyewitness testimony. Farmer's wife Nora Burnip, for example, said she was roused from her bed, sometime after midnight on January 5, by two sharp cracks. Yet miner James Golden, cycling home down the A182 around the same time neither heard nor saw anything out of the ordinary.

For the police version of event to be correct, the Mark X had to be parked, with a badly damaged front end, the rear driver's side window shot out and a dead man on the back seat, from around 12.30 onwards. Certainly, Sibbet had to be dead by midnight, at the very latest, if their case against Michael Luvaglio and Dennis Stafford was to stand any chance of success.

Yet as over thirty people, who had walked past the car testified, the car was not there at 12.10 and between 12.30 and 4.45 was reported as undamaged, with all the windows intact and no corpse sprawled across the back seat. For a full list of all these sightings, see the list below. Most of the passers-by were miners on their way to or from the colliery, but others include a bus driver, a lorry driver and a couple on their way home. None of them had any connection with the accused or any reason to perjure themselves on their behalf. All remembered the car because it was so unusual to see such an expensive vehicle in a village like South Hetton.

Sightings of Mark X

12.10 am - Mauro Terry reported no vehicle parked near Pesspool Bridge when he walked under it on his way to work in the colliery.

12.30 am - Mr. Ord sees dark coloured Mark X by the bridge and says it appeared undamaged.

12.35 am - Mr. Lee sees Mark X by the bridge and says it appeared undamaged.

12.45 am - Mr. McLeall (bus driver) sees Mark X by bridge. It appeared undamaged.

12.45 am - Mr. Forster sees Mark X by bridge. It appeared undamaged.

12.47am - Mr. Feather sees Mark X by bridge and is waved past by the driver who sticks his arm out of the driver's window.

12.55 am - Mr. Conroy sees Mark X by bridge. It appeared undamaged.

1.07 am - Mr. & Mrs. Robinson see Mark X facing opposite way. Slowed down and was certain there was no damage to front of car, all windows intact and front and rear seats empty.

1.10 am - Mr. Sturrock sees Mark X just before the bridge parked at an acute angle with the interior light on.

1.30am - Mr. Gibson reports no car parked near the bridge
1.40 am - Mr. Wilson sees Mark X parked near bridge. It appeared undamaged.
1.40 am - Mr. Sutton sees Mark X parked by bridge. It appeared undamaged.
1.50 am - Mr. Wood sees Mark X. Passenger near side front door open, footprints leading away in the snow. No damage to front of car. Felt heat rising from the bonnet, as if it had recently been driven. Claims to have opened the front passenger door but saw no body inside. Police did not find his fingerprints anywhere on the car.
1.55 am - Mr. McClement sees Mark X by bridge. No body and no signs of damage.
2.00 am - Jean Turnbull sees Mark X by bridge. No body and no damage.
2.00 am - Mr. Wharton sees Mark X by bridge. No body and no damage.
2.25 am - Mr. Purves, Mr. Simpson and Mr Howie see undamaged Mark X under bridge. Car empty and front offside headlight definitely not broken. Mr. Simpson claims to have run his hand along the entire length of car, but his fingerprints were not found on the vehicle later.
2.35 am - Joshua Leak sees Mark X by bridge. No body and no damage.
2.40 am - Mr. Quinn sees Mark X by bridge. No body and no damage.
2.40 am - Mr. Kitching sees Mark X by bridge. No body and no damage.
2.55 am - Mr. Wilson sees Mark X by bridge. It appeared undamaged.
2.55 am - Mr. Rutter sees Mark X by bridge. It appeared undamaged.
3.00 am - Mr. Oliver sees Mark X by bridge. It appeared undamaged.
3.20 am - Mr. Pickering sees Mark X by bridge. No body and no damage.
3.30 am - Mr. Hathaway sees Mark X by bridge. No body and no damage.
3.30 am - Mr. Wallace see Mark X by bridge. It appeared undamaged.
3.40 am - Mr. English sees Mark X by bridge. It appeared undamaged.

The Weakness of Eye-Witness Testimony
When it comes to eye-witness evidence an important caution is necessary. As American psychologist Elizabeth Loftus pointed out, in 1974, with the statement: 'I saw it with my own eyes, I can tell you exactly what happened,' carries a great deal of weight, with both police and jurors, and can make the difference between conviction and acquittal it should be treated with great care. Decades of psychological research has shown our memory, influenced as it is by expectations, values and cultural norms, is far from trustworthy. Studies of cases where a conviction depended on eyewitness identification, in the USA, for example, showed it was the leading cause of wrongful convictions. Subsequent DNA testing caused 72% of those verdicts to be overturned.
In her pioneering 'seventies study, Loftus demonstrated that eyewitness testimony can also be distorted by the way in which questions are posed. After being shown a video of two cars colliding, her subjects were asked: "About how fast were the cars going when they ****?

A different word or phrase was then used to fill in the blank. Some subjects were told the vehicles had 'smashed' into each other, others they 'collided', 'bumped', 'hit' or 'contacted'. She found that when 'smashed' was used speed was estimated at just over 40 miles an hour. When replaced by 'contacted' it fell to a little over 30 mph. [1]

Elizabeth Loftus suggested that two types of information are derived from witnessing a complex event. The first during the event and the second once the event is finished. These distort one another and create a single, specific, memory.

In a related experiment, it was found those told the cars had 'smashed' into each other were more likely to report seeing broken glass on the highway, even though there was none. [2]

Confusion over the speed of vehicles in this, and similar trials, may also be due to the fact that most people find it hard to judge, even under the best conditions, how fast a vehicle in travelling. When subjects were asked to estimate the speed of a car travelling at 12 mph, answers ranged from ten to fifty miles per hour. [3]

These are points to bear in mind when reviewing witness statements in this trial. We should also consider the possibility that some of the defence witnesses, were bribed to perjure themselves.

There is also the troubling possibility, to put it no higher, that damage to the Mark X had been deliberately exaggerated whilst in police custody at Peterlee. We have noted the anonymous letter claiming that the engine had been working perfectly when first started but was then deliberately run dry to support the police case. We also quoted the opinion of Jaguar engineer George Bowman that the hole in the radiator was more likely to have been made by a circular object such as a screwdriver, than any part of the E-Type. Finally, we have described how damage to the bonnet which the prosecution engineer Stanley Denton attributed to the collision had, in fact, been caused by the inappropriate method used for towing the heavy saloon.

Could all these seemingly independent and honest witness have been paid to perjure themselves? While this may seem pointless – how would their false testimony have assisted the police case. It is also most unlikely.

During the Appeal, Superintendent Kell alleged he had seen Vince Landa sitting in a nearby pub and handing out cash to these witnesses as they left the court. While Vince would have had no scruples about using bribery, it beggar's belief he would have done so immediately outside a courthouse surrounded by dozens of police. When asked by the judge what action he had

[1] Loftus, Elizabeth and Palmer, J.C (1974) Reconstruction of automobile destruction: An example of the interaction between language and memory. Journal of Verbal Learning and Verbal Behaviour, 13, 585–89
[2] Loftus, E. & Hoffman, H. (1989) Misinformation and Memory: The Creation of New Memories, Journal of Experimental Psychology General. University of Washington
[3] Marshall, J. (196) Law and psychology in conflict. New York: Anchor Books

taken about this, the Superintendent admitted he had done nothing. He gave no information about which of the witnesses Landa was bribing nor when. When presented with such clear evidence of wrongdoing he made no arrests.

Four Crucial Questions

The murder of Angus Sibbet raises four questions, all of which have to be addressed before a solution can be found.

How was he murdered?

Why was he murdered?

Who shot him?

Who ordered the killing?

Let's start by looking at how the killing *may* have taken place. We'll start with two assumptions. The first is that Michael Luvaglio and Dennis Stafford are innocent. The second that their account of the events of that night are honest and accurate.

Where Dennis is concerned there is every reason for doubting his word. A professional criminal and confidence trickster he is practised at deception. In 1980, for example, he managed to extract thousands from The News Of The World newspaper in the UK with a bogus confession to being the killer. A confession he took money from a rival tabloid, The People, to retract the following week.

Michael Luvaglio is a very different character. A lifelong Catholic who was led astray by the prospect of easy riches from his older brother's business acumen. He is a man who tells the truth no matter how grave the consequences for him. As we have seen, on two occasions, he turned down offers first to walk free immediately and second to have an early release from prison if he simply said he and Dennis had not been together at ny time that night.

If he is telling the truth, he and Dennis left Westmoreland Drive, Peterlee, in Landa's red E-Type, at approximately 11.30pm, not as early as 11pm, as claimed by Superintendents Kell and Mitchell. A departure time that is confirmed by Selena Jones, Pat Burgess, Lilian Bunker and solicitor Graham Andrews.

They then drove directly to Michael's home, in Chelsea Grove, Newcastle, to await a phone a call from Vince Landa in Majorca. This was confirmed by housewife Gladys Hill, who lived next door to Michael and Pat Morgan who clearly remembers seeing him on the phone, through the dining room window, and exchanging a wave

A third witness was company director Robert Anderson who garaged his car nearby and had walked past their house and saw the E-Type no later than 12.10.

After waiting around 15 minutes for the call, which never came, Michael and Dennis left for the Birdcage Club where they arrived about 12.20. This is confirmed by a number of witness, including doorman Matthew Dean, musicians John Michael McGarry, club manager John Bowden.

They left the sports car unlocked in an ally opposite the club where it was seen, undamaged, by Dorothy Brady at around 12.35. She claimed to have known it belonged to Vince Landa, as she had been employed to clean it. She also said that, when she left the club around 1.30, the car was no longer there.

Michael and Dennis remained in the club awaiting the arrival of Sibbet. Around 1.30, Michael telephoned Doreen Hall and asked if she knew where he was. About an hour later, Dennis left the Club to collect some duty-free cigarettes from the E-Type and found damage to its rear. This was confirmed by Matthew Dean. The car was, however, drivable and Michael and Dennis use it to drive back to Peterlee a short time later.

How Many Miles Did the E-Type Travel?

One further point should be made about the distance travelled by the E-Type on the night of January 4 and 5. The car had just been serviced so the current mileage would have been recorded by the garage, especially so since this was an almost new vehicle. It is easy to calculate the distance it would have travelled, during the period driven by Dennis Stafford under two conditions. The first is if he had done precisely what he claimed. Driven it from the garage to his home, then to the Birdcage Club in Stowell Street via Chelsea Grove, before driving back to Peterlee in the early hours. The following morning, he used it briefly before returning the car to the garage for repairs to the damaged rear. We calculate this to be around 70 miles. If the car had driven the route proposed by the police, there would have been more than a hundred added miles on the clock.

Did the police check the mileage when collecting the E-Type from Roker Car Sprays in Sunderland? If not, why not? And if they did why was this never used in evidence against the men? Presumably because the figures contradicted rather than supported their case.

If all these witnesses are correct, it cannot have been Landa's E-Type which was seen in convoy travelling along the A182 around the same time. Which must mean that a second red E-Type was involved. Why the killers should have evolved such a complex murder plan we will explain in a moment. But let's start by considering the likelihood of a duplicate sports car being involved.

Was There a Second Red E-Type?

Although no mention was made of a second E-Type during the trial, a surprise witness, called by the Prosecution during the Appeal in 1973, brought this possibility to the attention of the courts. At the time of the murder, William Potts Hall was a 19-year-old car mechanic who had made a statement to the police on the 7 January 1967 but had not been called to give evidence at the trial.

During the Appeal, Prosecutor Steven Cobb QC, asked the Court

President, Lord Chief Justice Widgery, for permission to call William Potts Hall whom he described as an important new witness. His presence had not been listed in the Court Papers or given to the Defence which led defence QC Cyril Hawser, to raise an objection. This was overruled by Lord Widgery and Potts Hall took the stand. Cobb asked him to listen as he read out the statement, he had made to Detective Sergeant Swan at Peterlee Police Station on January 8. (See copy of original statement below).

He had reported that, about 11 o'clock on the evening of Wednesday 4 January 1967, he had been walking home along Low Hills Road, Peterlee when he was passed by a red E-type Jaguar car coming from the direction of Westmorland Rise.'

50

Durham County Constabulary

_____ Division _____ Station _____ 8.1.67. ____ Date

STATEMENT FORM

Name and Address _____ William Potts HALL,
_____ 118 Westmorland Rise,
_____ Peterlee.

Age __19 yrs.__ Occupation _____ Mechanic.

I live at the above address with my parents.

About 11.00 p.m. on the evening of Wednesday, 4th January, 1967.

I was walking home along Low Hills Road, Peterlee, when I was passed

by a red 'E' type Jaguar car coming from the direction of Westmorland

Rise.

I couldn't say how many people were in the car or who was

driving.

(signed) W. P. Hall.

Statement taken at Peterlee Police Office at 11.15 a.m. 8.1.67. by
D/Sgt. 246 Swan.

Statement of William Potts Hall as written down by Detective Sergeant Swan on January 8, 1967

147

'Is that correct?' Steven Cobb asked him, clearly expecting confirmation. Instead, to the surprise of the court and the embarrassment of Mr Cobb, the young man shook in bewilderment before replying: 'No it is not correct. The date I saw a red E-Type was Saturday the 7th January, as I returned home from an evening out. I don't know why the police changed the statement, claiming that I saw the red E-Type on Wednesday 4th January.'

A clearly embarrassed Mr. Cobb attempted to retrieve the situation by suggesting the witness might, after all these years, be mistaken about the date he saw the red E-Type.

William Potts replied confidently: 'At the time I was a 19-year-old and a car enthusiast. I could not afford to go out in the evenings during the week, I only went out on Saturday nights.'

After which, Mr. Cobb could only apologise to the Lord Chief Justice and sit down in a state of confusion. Widgery asked Cyril Hawser if he had any questions. One might have expected the defence would seize this opportunity to further undermine the prosecution case. Landa's E-Type had been in the Peterlee police compound since Thursday, January 5. Two days before Mr. Potts Hall sighted a different E-Type on Saturday 7 January. Nor could either Michael or Dennis have been driving the other car since both men were in custody. This clearly gave rise to the suggestion of a second sports car being involved in the murder.

Rather than explore this possibility, Cyril Hawser replied: 'I do not wish to embarrass my learned colleague any more than is necessary. I have no questions to ask'.

If, as we believe likely, a second red E-Type was used why was this deemed necessary to the murder plot?

Did a 'Judas Jag' Lure Sibbet to his Death?

As we mentioned earlier, although Sibbet took considerable risks in his personal and working life, he was a cautious man who took great care to guard himself from his many enemies. He employed two bodyguards, Albert Ginley, full-time and another, Irish professional boxer called Paddy Hallett, as the need arose. He would have been unlikely to meet strangers in the middle of the night and in the countryside. As we explained, he had already avoided one such meeting in a deserted airfield, suspecting correctly it would end badly for him. He would, however, have been more than willing to drive out and meet Dennis and Michael, whom he trusted and whom he knew would be driving Landa's red E-Type that night. A second red E-Type could, therefore be used as what one witness we spoke to referred to as a 'Judas Jag', a decoy designed to lure an unsuspecting Sibbet to his death.

Sibbet's Last Message

Angus had been messaged while still at home, asking him to meet a 'Mick' at a

Workingman's Club in Shiney Row a village some twelve miles from Newcastle. Detectives later found a note, said to be in his handwriting, which read: 'Meeting 'Mick' at Shiney Row at 11.15' and intended for his mistress Joyce.

Shiney Row lies on the A 183 which links, via the B12841, to the A182. It was as the junction between these two roads that Police Constable John Ainsworth reported seeing a Mark X Jaguar turning right onto the main road and heading towards South Hetton. The time was shortly after 12.20. He also said the saloon was followed by a 'red mini with a white top' and thought the two vehicles were travelling together. This seems unlikely since no other witness saw this car which most likely had no connection with the case.

The possibility that this note had been left at her address, by Sibbet himself, between 11 and 11.30 that night was suggested by a plumber named David John Wood. He was a tenant in the multi-occupancy house in which Joyce lived with the doors of rooms facing one another across a narrow passageway. He had noticed Angus Sibbet visiting Joyce on several occasions over the previous months and knew that he drove a dark green Jaguar Mark X. He made a statement to the police that on the night of 4 January after he returned home from work at about 11.15. Ten minutes later he heard the sound of the front door opening. Taking a look, he saw the back of a large, broad shouldered man on his way out of the building and assumed this was Angus. Although, as he also made clear, only seeing him from behind he was unable to recognise him.

But if it was Sibbet, what was he doing leaving a note at around 11.15 saying he was meeting 'Mick' at that time miles away? If it was him, could the note have been one of his ploys to mislead Joyce as to he whereabouts? His presence miles from South Hetton at around 11.30 of course casts further doubts on the police version of events.

Because this note was hearsay evidence neither it nor the statement was never produced at the trial. As far as we know, the police never conducted any tests on the note to find out whether or not it was in Angus' handwriting.

The police assumed the note was intended for his mistress, Joyce Hall, and also believed that by 'Mick' he meant Michael Luvaglio and took this as confirmation the three were going to meet up. But, according to Luvaglio, Angus never called him 'Mick' always Michael. The one person who he did frequently refer to as Mick was Irishman Paddy Hallett. It looks like either someone purporting to be Hallett telephoned him or the ex-boxer told him personally in order to lure him into a trap. The latter is, it seems, is what Vince Landa believed and the reason why he decided to exact his revenge by having the former boxer run over a couple of weeks before the trial.

In the early hours of Friday, 17 February, Paddy Hallett had just left the Birdcage Nightclub, and was making his way across the nearby car park, when a Jaguar saloon was driven at him with the intention to kill or seriously injure him.

He managed to avoid the car which made two further, unsuccessful attempts. As the vehicle sped past, Hallett recognises the driver as Robert Knight Snowdon a former doorman at Vincent's Piccadilly club. Seated beside was another criminal he recognised, George Stewart. One of the two young men in the back of the car was Malcolm Tully. After the third attempt had been made to kill or injure him Hallett ran from the car park and fled across flower beds to prevent the car following him. It stopped and he heard footsteps behind him. Turning he saw Stewart running towards him and delivering a blow with his fist, which struck him in the face. His attacker then pulled out a knife and a fight followed during which Hallett was stabbed in the neck. A passing policeman intervened but while he was arresting Stuart, Hallett was attacked by Tully also armed with a knife. Detective Sergeant Heron, the Investigating Officer, believed the attackers were paid by Landa to deter him from giving evidence for the prosecution at Michael's trial

How Angus Sibbet Died

The following is one *possible* account of the events leading up to the murder of Angus. He had received a message which either came from Paddy Hallett or purported to come from him. What exactly this message was we will never know. Presumably, for Sibbet to have turned out on a cold January night and driven all that way to Shiney Row it must have been something which threatened his wealth. Social Club Services had installed four fruit machines in the village's workingmen's club, and he may have been told that one of the committee members had been caught fiddling the machines and needed a firm talking to. We shall never know.

What we do know is that, at 11.15, Angus left La Dolce Vita, meeting up with photographer Tom Oxley on his way out. They chatted briefly as he paid for his photographs, he may then have driven to Joyce Hall's flat before going on to Shiney Road where he arrived at around 11.45. Whether or not he entered the club we do not know.

If the police interviewed anyone in the club to check whether or not he had turned up, their notes have been lost or destroyed. This was something Kell was particularly keen to authorise as soon as he was able. In less than a year after Stafford and Luvaglio had been sentenced, he ordered all the evidence disposed of. On September 14, 1968, he wrote the note overleaf to the Chief Constable:

To: Chief Constable.

I have spoken to Mr. Palmes of the D.P.P's office and he agrees with me that as LUVAGLIO and STAFFORD cannot take their Appeal any further, no useful purpose would be served by the Police retaining the exhibits in this case any further.

I have arranged with D/Sgt. Morgan that all the exhibits are to be returned to their owners, where necessary/and the remainder are to be retained by as and will form a display, to be housed in the museum.

14.9.68.   Superintendent.

Note from Superintendent Kell to the Chief Constable, dated September 1969

This was a lie. Scarcely any the material was returned to the owners and there never was any such institution as the police 'museum.' All the evidence, including blood samples and fingerprints, were destroyed.

Inside the E-Type
Frustrated by his wasted journey to the Shiney Row club, Sibbet decided to drive the four miles to the A182 and meet Michael and Dennis as they drove towards Newcastle. What he did not know was that he was already being followed by two men in a red E-type. They made no attempt to come closer to the Mark X until the two cars were heading towards South Hetton. For one thing they did not want to spook their victim by making him realise he must have been followed from Newcastle. For another, a red mini with a white roof had slotted itself in between themselves and the saloon.

It was shortly after midnight that the two cars, now close together and with the E-Type in the lead, sped past cyclist James Golden without stopping. They then swung right into Pesspool Lane. Sibbet believing the two men in the sports car were Michael and Dennis followed them into the darkness of the unlit lane. Not far from the junction the E-type stopped abruptly and Sibbet pulled up a short distance behind.

Angus only realised the danger he was in as he saw, with horror, it was not Michael and Dennis clambering from the sports car but another man instead together with a tall stranger. Although for legal reasons we cannot name this man, we can say that he was also involved in the assault on Paddy Hallett in the incident we described earlier.

Frantically attempting to escape, he accelerated and turned the wheel hard right in a vain attempt to get away. The two cars collided, although not especially violently. This caused only a small amount of damage to the saloon's radiator and the rear of the sports car. In doing so, he caught the stranger a glancing blow on the right leg with his bumper.

Sibbet then flung open the door and ran towards the men as if to attack them. As he did so, the injured stranger fired four times. The first bullet went wide, smashing his car's rear window. The other three entered his body at point-blank range. One severed the aorta and he was dead as he hit the ground, falling heavily onto the grass verge grazing his face as he did so.

The two men then dragged Sibbet's lifeless corpse across the wet and muddy grass. Opening both of the Mark X's rear doors, with one standing on the verge and the other on the lane, they manhandled his body onto the back seat, leaving their fingerprints on both these doors while doing so.

They now had a dead and bloodied man on their hands and a problem. The intention of the man who had ordered the attack on Sibbet was to frame Vince Landa for the murder. He had hoped the circumstantial evidence of the two cars driving in convoy through a busy mining village, would be sufficient to bring him under suspicion. Possibly even to have him charged with the murder. What he did not know was Vincent was back in Majorca at the hospital bedside of his teenage son.

The killers' problem was unless the E-type, parked outside The Birdcage Club, showed similar damage Landa would be in the clear. While they debated their next move, the two men smoked, leaving the cigarette stubs on the verge.

After a brief, panic stricken discussion they gathered up as much of the evidence as they could find, including the bullet cases and parts of the damaged rear light cover from the E-type and put them into the sports car. The local criminal drove the vehicle back onto the A182 and along the road until he was opposite West Moor Farm. There, at around 12.20, he fired two shots before scattering the collision debris over the verge. He was then supposed to return and collect the Cockney gunman but lost his nerve and sped back to garage from which he had earlier collected the E-Type. On the 7th January another associate arranged for the broken rear light to be repaired and the E-Type driven back to London by night.

While this scenario may sound implausible, it seems the only way to explain the shots Nora Burnip heard and why there were only two of them when three were used in Sibbet's murder. As we have established it could not have been carried out at the time and in the manner the police claimed, as this would fly in the face of cyclist Golden's evidence.

The gunman waited a short while, smoking to calm his nerves, before driving the Mark X along the deserted country lane. He expected to meet the local man along the way, abandon the car and corpse in the middle of the empty countryside and return with him to Newcastle. When this never happened, he had no choice but to return to South Hetton where he suspected, correctly, there was a phone box from which he could call for help.

Arriving in the mining village, he parked the Mark X close to Pesspool Bridge and made his call to The Birdcage Club from a box outside the Post Office, which was not far away. When manhandling Sibbet's body he had got blood on his hands and was also bleeding from the injury to his right calf. It was this blood he inadvertently smeared on the interior of the saloon while leaving Sibbet's blood on a page of the telephone directory.

The gunman also telephoned his employer, angry at being stranded in a small mining village with a bleeding leg, a collision damaged saloon and a body on the back seat. He was told to stay put, keep calm and he would sort out everything. Somewhat pacified, the gunman decided he would be better off sitting in the warmth of the Mark X than standing conspicuously by the side of the road and freezing in the snow which was, by then, falling quite heavily. While this was a risk it was not a serious one. The radiator damage was fairly slight and not immediately obvious. The rear window although shattered, looked to a casual observer, as if it had simply been left open.

The killer was still in the car, smoking a cigar, at 12.47 when he waved on bus driver Mr Thomas Feather. Shortly afterwards, perhaps realising how many people would likely be walking past the car and fearing capture, the gunman left the vehicle and started walking back along the A182 towards Newcastle. About a mile from Pesspool Bridge, at the junction with the B1284, he met his driver. 29 year-old John Tumblety, also known as 'Scotch Johnny', who had driven from Newcastle to give him a lift back to the Birdcage Club. Tumblety's departure from the Club and his return, about an hour later in the company of the Cockney, was confirmed by doorman Matthew Dean.

Who was Tumblety and why should he have agreed to risk of involving himself in a murder by giving a lift to the killer?

John Tumblety

Well known in criminal circles as a good getaway driver Tumblety, who had been in and out of prison most of his adult life, was a small-time crook from Edinburgh who liked to hang around with big time villains. A familiar face in the Birdcage Club, he was sufficiently trusted by management to leave stolen jewellery in their safe. During one robbery Tumblety had stumbled across a private collection of handguns, including a Beretta and Walther pistols. These he stole and hired out to criminals wanting a weapon. It was one of these guns that was used to shoot Sibbet. Which explains why he was so willing to collect the gunman from South Hetton.

The gang boss who had ordered the killing had one further task to organise. Now that the two cars had accidentally collided, it was essential for Landa's E-Type to suffer from similar collision damage to the rear. Fortunately, this man's boss who had driven down from Glasgow to supervise the shooting owned a Mark X Jaguar. A vehicle he had previously used to kill two young Glaswegians, Patrick Welsh and James Goldie who had argued with one of the bookies he protected over a trivial sum of money. It was a simple matter for him to drive his saloon into the rear of the E-type, still parked outside the Birdcage Club.

Around eight, the following morning, the gunmen turned up at the Fleet Buyers Garage, in Whessoe Road, Darlington owned by brothers Colin and Stuart Dunn, associates of Vince Landa. The only worker to have arrived that early was freelance paint sprayer named Tom Fellows who was renting that part of the garage off Colin Dunn. He described how an agitated man in his early 30s, speaking with a Cockney accent, came into the garage and demanded to speak with the owner. The man, had black, slicked-back hair with a widow's peak, a broken nose which had been reset and a distinctive scar on his forehead. He introduced himself as Darren Reynolds. The man, who was holding an automatic pistol, had a badly injured right leg which he claimed had been crushed between his car and the Mark X belonging to Angus Sibbet.

'He told me he'd been ordered to frighten Mr Sibbet but had feared the heavily built collector was about to attack him so had shot him dead.' He told us. 'I thought why broadcast it if you've just killed someone? I just stared at him. I think he thought I was one of the mob. I asked: 'Do you want me to phone for an ambulance?' He yelled 'no'. He was very anxious. He was perspiring and I could see the beads of sweat on his forehead. He told me he'd been told to go to the garage if anything went wrong and repeated 'where the hell is Colin?' He loosened off a shot into asbestos cladding on some piping running along the wall and began waving the gun in my face. My reaction was to put my arms in front of my face and duck down like a boxer.'

A few minutes later Colin Dunn arrived and led the gunman away, warning Fellows: 'That man's never been here'.

Fears for his own safety initially prevented Fellows from reporting the incident to the police. He finally did so, six years later, after seeing media coverage of a forthcoming Court of Appeal bid by Luvaglio and Stafford in 1973. 'I went to Darlington Police Station, but the detective taking the statement was hostile, threatening to arrest me for wasting police time. I walked home totally shattered at the degrading experience," he said.

Although Tom Fellows' statement was never passed to defence barristers for Luvaglio and Stafford at the time of the appeal, it was mentioned in a 2007 Criminal Case Review Commission (CCRC) examination of the case. However, it was rejected because it did not fit with other evidence and because police claimed that Mr Fellows had a business arrangement with Vince Landa. Fellows denied this, explaining the only time he had had any dealings with Landa was when he examined a sick horse belonging to the entrepreneur at his home at Dryderdale Hall. He also pointed out that, although the garage has since been knocked down, it stood for many years after he made his statement and police could have easily confirmed his account by searching for the bullet fired by the man. The police never attempted to interview Colin Dunn regarding Mr Fellows' statement.

'I'm not bothered if anyone believes me or not', Tom Fellows says. 'I can't prove if this man killed him or not – I'm just saying that this is what happened to me.'

The Man Who Shot Angus Sibbet
In 2013 Tom Fellows with police artist Jan Szymczuk created a portrait of the man who visited him in Colin Dunn's garage in January 1967. Together they created the image below, a likeness of the gang member who murdered Angus Sibbet on the pitch dark, freezing, January night in 1967.
Who is he? The consensus of opinion, among those who either belonged to or were close to London's sixties' gangsters, he closely resembles Albert Donoghue, Reggie Kray's right-hand man. Below we have placed his photograph alongside the composite sketch to illustrate the likeness.
A further overlay image appears in the photograph section of this book.

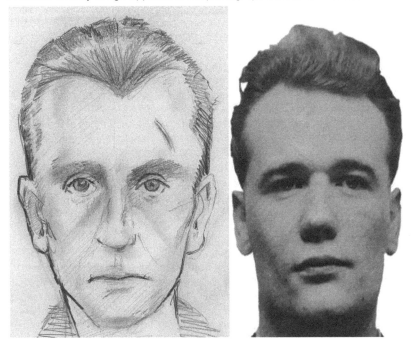

Portrait of a murderer? How Tom Fellows remembers the man who called himself Darren Reynolds, as drawn by ex-Metropolitan Police artist Jan Szymczuk (Photograph Media Arts).
Beside it a photograph of Albert Donoghue from around the same period.

The Violent Life of Albert Donoghue
Albert Donoghue was born in Dublin, on Bonfire Night 1935, to a strict working-class catholic family. His father, Joe, was in the British Merchant Navy and, when Albert was three, moved the family to London's East End. A few months later he caught pneumonia and died. At the outbreak of war his mother married John Barry, another Irishman, with whom she had eight more children. As an adult, Donoghue would sometimes use the name Barry to confuse the authorities.

When the Blitz started, he was evacuated, together with his brothers and sisters to Devon and later went to a strict Catholic boarding school in Orpington, Kent. But the frequent beating and constant preaching did nothing to quell his rebellious and violent nature. By the age of fifteen he was in Wormwood Scrubs, at the start of a long period in the Borstal system. A tall boy for his age, he earned the nickname 'Big' Albert, joining the Merchant Navy as a deckhand in 1953. His period of honest work did not last long. By twenty-one he had embarked on a life of crime starting with payroll snatches and operating from the London district of Bow, two miles east of the Krays territory in Bethnal Green. By the late 1950's he was working at the racecourses on behalf of Billy Hills lieutenant, Albert Dimes. At the age of 21 he met his 17-year-old wife to be. They married soon after. On February 25, 1958, he was convicted of factory breaking with intent and went to prison for fifteen months.

His sister-in-law was married to Billy Donovan, a member of the Kray Firm and doorman at the Double R Club, owned by Ronnie and Reggie. This brought him into his first contact with the Twins. Albert was a good friend of a man called Lenny Hamilton who fell out with Ronnie Kray and was tortured by him with a red-hot poker. Afterwards he refused to tell anybody who had burned him so badly. Not knowing the perpetrator, Albert was heard to say: 'If they'd done that to me, I'd have blown their heads off.'

On the 17th September 1962 he was given a three-year prison sentence after being found guilty of involvement in a £3,000 payroll robbery and sent to Pentonville prison. Ronnie, on learning what Donoghue had said took this as a threat. On Albert's release from prison, in October 1964, he was sent a message from the Krays asking for a meeting in the Crown and Anchor in Bethnal Green. While drinking at the bar, Albert noticed other customers people moving quickly away from him. Before he could react, Reggie shot him in the back of the leg. When he came out of hospital, he was told to come and see the twins at their home in Vallance Road. As a reward for demonstrating his loyalty, by refusing the say anything to the police about the shooting, the Krays put him on a pension and later found him a place on the Firm. Later he became their enforcer and paymaster, the 'face of the gang' who worked alongside them through their most violent years.

In 1966, he played a vital role in the escape of 'Mad Axemen', Frank Mitchell, from Dartmoor prison. His job was to take supplies to the flat where

Mitchell was being held and set him up with a young hostess named Liza to keep him happy.

Despite Albert's best efforts, Mitchell became increasingly restless and angry. He demanded to be allowed to visit family and meet old friends. After he threatened to visit the Twins at their Vallance Road home, Ronnie decided he was too much of a trouble and asked Freddie Foreman, an old friend from South London to 'sort out' the Mitchell situation.

In December 1966 Foreman and, Alfie Gerrard arrived in a van and Albert, who had arrived before them, promised Mitchell he was being taken to spend Christmas with Reggie and Ronnie. Once inside the van, Foreman and Gerrard shot him a dozen times at point-blank range and let him bleed to death. Fearing that, as the only witness, he would be the next to be shot Albert told the men to drop him off near his home. From there he phoned Reggie, telling him 'that dog has won.' This was the signal that Frank Mitchell was dead. He was then tasked with making sure that Lisa would keep her mouth shut. After assuring her she would be safe he took her back to his own flat and spent the night with her. He later admitted that had the girl appeared to pose any threat to the Krays then she too would have been shot.

There was no job so dirty that Albert was not prepared to do it for his friends the Krays as well as for any of their friends. After Reggie stabbed another gangster, Jack 'the Hat' McVite through the throat, killing him outright and coating the murder scene with blood, Donoghue cleaned and redecorated it for him.

In late December 1966, he was sent to Newcastle to 'put the fear of God' into Angus Sibbet. There was no intention, on Vince Landa's part to kill him merely to prove a warning. Seeing the big, burly and extremely angry Angus charging towards him, Donoghue panicked and fired the fatal shots. Following the killing he informed the Twins about what had happened.

Four months later, on May 8, 1968, the Krays were arrested. When Albert was allowed to see Reggie in police custody, he was ordered by him to confess to Frank Mitchell's murder. Increasingly appalled by their readiness to inflict violence, Donoghue refused. As well as Mitchell and McVite, Ronnie had gunned down a member of the rival Richardson gang, George Cornell, in the Blind Beggar public house. Rather than do as ordered, Donoghue went to the police and told them everything he knew. His frank and detailed description of the Twins violence and criminality led to them spending the next thirty years behind bars. He did not, however, say anything about murdering Angus Sibbet since this would have, undoubtedly, led to a lengthy prison sentence.

Albert Donoghue, the man who shot Angus Sibbet and played a key a major role in the rise of one of Britain's most brutal criminal gangs also played a major part in their ultimate destruction. But if Donoghue pulled the trigger who ordered him to do so?

With the Krays now more or less out of action, and living in isolation in their luxurious Suffolk mansion, it seems unlikely they were directly involved. Far more likely, that for a suitable finder's fee, they merely pointed 'Vince, in the direction of their most trusted lieutenant Albert and also suggested he contact a close associate of theirs, an equally violent professional criminal living in Scotland. His name was Arthur Thompson, but for thirty years he as better known on his home territory as the 'Godfather of Glasgow'

The Life and Crimes of Arthur Thompson

Thompson started his criminal career as a moneylender, aged nineteen, and rapidly built a terrifying reputation for violence. He crucified anyone who failed to repay a loan on time, nailing their hands and feet to a floor or door. From loan sharking he expanded into protection rackets. It was rumoured that, by the early 1990's the Thompson family were earning some hundreds of thousand pounds a week from these criminal activities.

A shrewd businessman Arthur had, from the start, invested his money in legitimate businesses. These did so well that, by the start of the 'sixties, he had become one of the wealthiest men in Scotland.

In 1966 he narrowly escaped death when a bomb exploded under his car. His mother-in-law, in the passenger seat, died instantly. Shortly afterwards, he spotted the two men he suspected of the planting the bomb, Patrick Welsh and Eddy Pumphrey, from a rival gang. They were driving together in a van. Using his Mark X as a weapon, he forced them off the road. The van struck a lamppost killing both men outright. The incident was witnessed by two police officers and Thompson was arrested and charged with murder. When no other witnesses were prepared to testify against him, the case was dropped.

Like all greedy men, Thompson was always hungry to gain more money, power and influence. Which is why he was interested when his old friend Ronnie Kray sent a messenger to Glasgow with a proposition.

If he would help frame Vince Landa for the murder of one of his associates, Social Club Services would collapse and the two of them could take control of a business worth millions. All he had to do was provide a driver who knew the area and Ronnie would send up one of his best men to take care of the rest.

Thompson agreed and even offered to drive down to Newcastle to keep an eye on things. When Donoghue reported that Sibbet was dead, but there had been a collision between his Mark X and the duplicate E-Type, Thompson easily resolved matters by motoring to Stowell Street and driving his own Jaguar into the rear of Landa's sports car.

The plan work better than they could have ever hoped. The Public Offering collapsed as soon as Stafford and Luvaglio were arrested. Social Club Services went out of business within weeks, allowing the Kray's and Thompson family to take over Landa's collapsed Fruit Machine empire.

While this must remain speculation, the involvement of Arthur Thompson in the killing was widely rumoured by both London and Scotland's underworld. Among these was Frankie Fraser, a notorious South London gangster. Fraser was so certain Thompson had been involved, that he went public with the accusation in the 'seventies.

The Role of Vince Landa'
Why should Vince have arranged for his long-time business partner and old friend to receive, as he expected, a beating? As we explained earlier, Landa had every reason to feel betrayed by his old friend and partner Angus Sibbet. Not only was the man stealing from him on a weekly basis but had, as we explained earlier, once attempted to frighten him from coming back to England with a forged letter purporting to be from Durham police. This plot had failed after Vince phoned a police contact and learned no such letter had been sent. But Sibbet still had detailed knowledge of Landa's responsibility for the hit-and-run killing and was threatening to make this public unless Landa increased his share of the hugely lucrative public offering.

Vince used his brief post-Christmas stopover in London, to hire some suitable 'muscle' for the job and organise a red E-type similar to his own. This presented no problems for him since he was already running a thriving motorcar sales business and so had plenty of contacts in the trade. This business involved exporting Minis to America and importing luxury American Cadillacs and Pontiac's. Through his contacts he would have had no trouble in locating the car he needed in order to lull Sibbet into a full sense of security. He made sure he was out of the country when the attack took place, using his sick son as a reason to fly back to Majorca.

If Angus ever complained to the police about the attack, which Vincent thought most unlikely, he had no reason to fear that his brother and Dennis would be implicated. Both had cast-iron alibis, being seen by numerous witnesses drinking and eating in the Birdcage Club at the time. What he had failed to reckon with was Sibbet using his Mark X to injure Albert Donohue causing him to panic and shoot Sibbet dead by accident. On returning with the gunman to the Birdcage, an aggrieved gunman ordered John Tumblety to drive his saloon into the back of the E-Type, perhaps in an attempt to implicate Landa whom he blamed for things going so wrong.

Michael flatly refutes the idea his older brother was involved. He points out, reasonably, that his brother was very unlikely to do something as rash when both were about to earn so much money when the business went public.

What we know for sure is that while on remand in prison, Michael had a visit from his brother. On the pretext of providing him with the best possible defence, he persuaded him to sign over all his shares in Social Club Services, assuring him it was only temporary. They were never returned. While he had worshipped the ground Vince walked on as a child, Michael refused to have anything to do with him after his brother had fleeced him. It was Michael's decision to not keep in touch, rather than Vince's. By the time Vince died Michael had also found out the anguish Vince had put his parents through while he was inside and that reinforced his decision not to go to Vince's funeral.

Chapter Fifteen: After the Trial Was Over

'Now I'm going to make another million. But it could take me until the end of this year.'
Vince Landa in 1980

Immediately after the trial, Vince Landa fled abroad to escape arrest and remained out of the country, living mostly in Spain and Italy, for the next thirteen years. During his time on the run he was able to slip in and out of Britain on at least three occasions to visit friends and family in Sunderland. He always travelled to England by public transport never on his 180-ton yacht, The Joy of Lee, which he kept in the Mediterranean where he went on cruises with his friends from the North.

In 1969 he was arrested by a Madrid judge and jailed while the authorities waited for an extradition order to arrive from Britain. But, even in Spain, Landa still had powerful friends in high places and plenty of money with which to ensure justice was done. After three months languishing behind bars, he was abruptly released from prison. No explanation was given to the British Embassy. He returned to his family to continue his comfortable lifestyle in a large and luxurious villa near Palermo.

By the mid-seventies, he had broken up with his wife and family. 'I have a common law wife now,' he told a reporter in 1977. 'We have spent most of our time together in Greece, but she had a nervous breakdown and is now in London.'

In 1977, he took The Joy of Lee to Sicily hoping to find work on oil rigs owned by Eni, the Italian state oil company. In December that year he was arrested in Syracuse on fraud charges.

'I was put in solitary confinement and treated badly at first,' he told a reporter who had flown out from Newcastle to interview him. 'But when they found out who I was they treated me well.'

Released on payment of a fine, he left prison to find that his yacht had sunk under mysterious circumstances. He told his insurance company the propeller had caught in a fishing net breaking the stern tube and flooding the vessel. The company investigated the loss but refused to pay out.

Vincent was approached by a film director and asked to become a technical adviser in a film they were making of a film about his extraordinary and eventful life. He readily and an announcement was made at the Cannes Film Festival that the venture had sufficient funding to go ahead. It was about to start production when the producer and script writer, North East journalist Patrick Lavelle, died from cancer. The project collapsed.

In January 1980, he finally returned to England to stand trial, having been assured he would not be sent to prison. In February, Teesside Crown Court was told by the prosecution that he had contracted to provide clubs with new Fruit Machines but supplied them with old ones. He had guaranteed them a £40 a month profit but collected all their takings and took a 50% rake off from the hire purchase company. He pleaded guilty to seven fraud charges and was fined £2,750 with £1,000 costs.

Leaving the court with his new fiancée, 19-year-old Julie Hamblin and daughters, Dawn and Claire, at his side he told journalists: 'Now I'm going to make another million. But it could take me until the end of this year.'

The following year he opened the Castle Inn, a pub and restaurant which had cost him £50,000 and taken nine months to refurbish. For a short while the business proved successful. Then, in July 1981 it was devastated by fire and permanently closed.

Fire seemed to follow Vince Landa around. Long after he had relinquished ownership, Dryderdale Hall was also severely damaged in an arson attack. The same year he was declared bankrupt. From then on it was all downhill financially for the man who had once been praised in Newcastle as a 'Legend'.

On June 27, 2011, he died suddenly, from a pulmonary embolism, alone in his one bedroom Essex flat. He was seventy-six and lay dead in his apartment for over a week before being found.

Michael and Dennis were released in 1979, after serving 12 years they remain on licence subject to recall to jail at a moment's notice

After leaving prison Michael, a devout Catholic, spent the next twenty-five years working for London based SHARE - Self Help and Rehabilitation for Employment. Established in 1972, the charity's aim is to transform the lives of people with a disability, including learning difficulties, autism and mental health needs. His charitable work has been recognised with several awards, including in a letter from the Queen. Due to his prison record he was prevented from receiving an OBE. Now in his mid-eighties and in very poor health, he continues to protest his innocence and has offered a substantial reward, £50,000 ($63,569) to anyone who can clear his name.

Dennis Stafford went back into business with Landa, buying the eighteenth-century Stanhope Castle, some thirty miles outside Newcastle. Their relationship turned sour after Vince was declared bankrupt. In 2009 Dennis was acquitted of threatening to set fire to a car, which subsequently was destroyed in an arson attack, causing damage to Stanhope Castle.

In July 1983, he was arrested on forgery charges. A court heard how he and East End printer Peter Baranowski planned to flood the market with half a million pounds worth of bogus American Express Travellers Cheques. Stafford, who now called himself Dennis Scott, was sentenced to six years imprisonment and Baranowski to five.

Ronald Kell was promoted to Chief Superintendent soon after the Sibbet murder trial, Kell was made Sunderland police chief in August 1969. In 1976, aged 54, he retired from the force and died peacefully on January 28, 2013 at the age of ninety-one. On his retirement Kell was awarded the Queen's Police Medal in recognition of his long and distinguished service ensuring wrongdoers ended up behind bars. Whatever it took to put them there.